Benefiting from Life's Trials

Benefiting from Life's Trials

by
John MacArthur, Jr.

WORD OF GRACE COMMUNICATIONS
P.O. Box 4000
Panorama City, CA 91412

All Scripture quotations, unless noted otherwise, are from the *New Scofield Reference Bible,* King James Version. Copyright © 1967 by Oxford University Press, Inc. Reprinted by permission.

Library of Congress Cataloging in Publication Data

MacArthur, John, 1939-
    Benefiting from life's trials / by John MacArthur, Jr.
       p.   cm.   (John MacArthur's Bible studies)
    Includes indexes.
    ISBN 0-8024-5356-2
    1. Bible. N.T. James I, 1-18—Criticism, interpretation, etc.
  2. Temptation—Biblical teaching. I. Title. II. Series:
MacArthur, John, 1939-   Bible studies.
BS2785.2.M24   1988
248.8'6—dc19   87-31019
                                              CIP

1 2 3 4 5 6 7 8 Printing/LC/Year 93 92 91 90 89 88

Printed in the United States of America

Contents

These Bible studies are taken from messages delivered by Pastor-Teacher John MacArthur, Jr., at Grace Community Church in Panorama City, California. These messages have been combined into a 6-tape album entitled *Benefiting from Life's Trials*. You may purchase this series either in an attractive vinyl cassette album or as individual cassettes. To purchase these tapes, request the album *Benefiting from Life's Trials*, or ask for the tapes by their individual GC numbers. Please consult the current price list; then, send your order, making your check payable to:

WORD OF GRACE COMMUNICATIONS
P.O. Box 4000
Panorama City, CA 91412

Or call the following toll-free number:
1-800-55-GRACE

1
The Purpose of Trials

Outline

Introduction
A. The Testing of Abraham
   1. The request
   2. The response
   3. The result
      a) Abraham's obedience
      b) The angel's interruption
B. The Appraisal of Abraham

Lesson
 I. Trials Test the Strength of Our Faith
    A. The Example of Hezekiah
    B. The Example of Habakkuk
    C. The Example of Job
 II. Trials Humble Us
III. Trials Wean Us from Worldly Things
    A. Explained
    B. Exemplified
       1. By Jesus
       2. By Moses
IV. Trials Call Us to an Eternal Hope
    A. Stated
    B. Supported
       1. Romans 8
       2. 2 Corinthians 4
 V. Trials Reveal What We Really Love
    A. Stated
    B. Supported
       1. Deuteronomy 13:3
       2. Luke 14:26-27

Introduction

Going through any trial in life can be a joyous experience for a Christian if his perspective is right. Imagine the worst trial you could possibly face. For some of you it might be financial crisis, accompanied by the loss of your savings. For others it might be the loss of employment, with the resulting loss of dignity in being unable to support your family. Perhaps it might be the announcement of a serious illness in your family, a fatal car accident, or the manifestation of evil in the form of rape, murder, or robbery. Some of those tragic events have touched or will touch us or our families in one way or another.

The book of Job reminds us that trouble is inevitable: "Man is born unto trouble, as the sparks fly upward" (5:7). Anyone who tries to create a fantasy world where everything is perfect is setting himself up for profound sorrow. Unfortunately, the anticipation of sorrow and trouble often casts a shadow over our greatest joys. Maybe that's the reason Scripture records Jesus weeping but never laughing. Perhaps Jesus did laugh on occasion, but I believe His happiness was offset by His overwhelming sadness over sin.

All of us, to some degree or another, are going to have to look in the eyes of agony at some point in our lives. We need to understand how to face the trials that will come. Job encountered some of the severest trials imaginable. He lost his children and his livestock. His body was afflicted with painful boils. And, worse, he was left with a wife who offered no sympathy. But in my judgment, the person who faced the severest trial of any human was Abraham.

A. The Testing of Abraham

Genesis 22 describes the test God gave Abraham. I believe we can learn from Abraham's example.

1. The request

"It came to pass . . . that God did test Abraham, and said unto him, Abraham: and he said, Behold, here I am. And he said, Take now thy son, thine only son Isaac, whom thou lovest, and get thee into the land of Moriah; and offer him there for a burnt offering upon one of the mountains which I will tell thee of" (vv. 1-2).

God's request did not fit in with Abraham's theology. In the covenant of God there was no history of human sacrifice; that was a pagan practice. No child of God offered his own kind in sacrifice. Furthermore, Isaac was the son of promise. God had touched the loins of Abraham and Sarah and enabled them to produce a son who would be an integral part in fulfilling God's covenant with Abraham.

Why would God call for a human sacrifice when He never called for one before? It didn't make sense for God to miraculously enable a barren woman to produce a son and then later ask that he be killed. Why would God promise Abraham that he would be the father of many nations (Gen. 12:1-3) and then ask him to kill his only child? All hope of progeny and promise would die, which would strike a blow at the covenant faithfulness of God. What makes this the severest trial imaginable is not that Isaac was to die but that Abraham was to kill Isaac with his own hand. It's one thing to be told the one you love will die, but it's something else to be told to kill that person. If anything God commanded ever deserved a lengthy argument, this was it. We might have expected Abraham to say, "This makes no sense. I can't do it. Could you please explain Yourself?"

2. The response

"Abraham rose up early in the morning, and saddled his ass, and took two of his young men with him, and Isaac his son, and cut the wood for the burnt offering, and rose up, and went unto the place of which God had told him. Then on the third day Abraham lifted up his eyes, and saw the place afar off. And Abraham said to his young men, abide ye here with the ass; and I and the lad will go yonder and worship, and come again to you. And Abraham took the wood of the burnt offering, and laid it upon Isaac his son; and he took the fire in his hand, and a knife; and they went both of them together. And Isaac spoke unto Abraham, his father, and said, My father: and he said, Here am I, my son. And he said, Behold the fire and the wood: but where is the lamb for a burnt offering? And Abraham said, My son, God will provide himself a lamb for a burnt offering: so they went both of them together" (vv. 3-8).

Abraham, without questioning or arguing, immediately obeyed God's request. Abraham demonstrated amazing faith in telling his servants that both he and his son would return, and in telling his trusting son that God would provide the sacrifice. I believe that deep in his heart Abraham knew God had something in mind consistent with His character and His covenant.

3. The result

a) Abraham's obedience

"They came to the place which God had told him of; and Abraham built an altar there, and laid the wood in order, and bound Isaac, his son, and laid him on the altar upon the wood. And Abraham stretched forth his hand, and took the knife to slay his son" (vv. 9-10).

What unbelievable faith! Now you understand both the nature of faith that God reckons as righteousness (Gen. 15:6) and why Paul identified Abraham as the father of the faithful (Rom. 4:11-12). Apart

10

from Christ, Abraham is our greatest role model for trusting in God. He is the epitome of submission and obedience to the will of God at any cost. And God honored that, as the next verses show.

b) The angel's interruption

"The angel of the Lord called unto him out of heaven, and said, Abraham, Abraham: and he said, Here am I. And he said, Lay not thine hand upon the lad, neither do thou anything unto him, for now I know that thou fearest God, seeing thou hast not withheld thy son, thine only son from me" (vv. 11-12).

This was a test to determine if Abraham would obey God, and Abraham passed. This account shows that we might be tested in the things most near and dear to us. We may have to offer up our own Isaacs—the ones we love most—and give them to the Lord. Like Abraham, we must be willing to give up what is most precious to us. We must be ready to do anything God asks us to do, knowing that He is all-wise.

We all face many trials in life, but I can't imagine experiencing a trial like Abraham's. His obedience took a tremendous amount of self-denial and therefore was of the highest degree of excellence. Abraham passed the test. That was confirmed when the angel of the Lord said, "Now I know that thou fearest God" (v. 12). Abraham reverenced God at the highest cost.

B. The Appraisal of Abraham

The commentary on this trial of Abraham is given in Hebrews 11. Here we learn what enabled Abraham to pass such a test: "By faith Abraham, when he was tested, offered up Isaac; and he that had received the promises offered up his only begotten son, of whom it was said, In Isaac shall thy seed be called; accounting [taking note of the fact] that God was able to raise him up, even from the dead" (vv. 17-19). Abraham was willing to obey God because he believed God could raise the dead, even though

11

he had never before seen the dead raised to life. He believed God was so true to His Word and character that if He made a promise, He would even raise the dead to keep it. That is an example of tremendous faith. Is it any wonder he is the greatest human model of faith? Galatians 3 says, "They who are of faith, the same are the sons of Abraham. . . . They who are of faith are blessed with faithful Abraham" (vv. 7, 9). Anyone who lives by faith in God is in a spiritual sense a son of Abraham. He is the father of the faithful. The account of Abraham tells us that a man can go through the severest trial of life imaginable if he trusts God, believing that He will keep His promise and accomplish His purposes without making a mistake.

We have to realize that God is going to allow us to go through tests and that He is working all things out for His own holy purpose (Rom. 8:28). I know we all dream of a perfect environment of comfort and tranquillity. Although any temporary rest from trials may lead us into believing we might find permanent exemption from them, our lives on earth will never be free from trials. David reflected that truth when he said, "In my prosperity I said, I shall never be moved" (Ps. 30:6). We can live in a fool's paradise, never forecasting any trouble and predicting a future of ease, but that is a fantasy. Christ warned His disciples and all who follow in His footsteps to expect trials in this life (John 15:18–16:6).

Puritan Thomas Manton once observed that God had one Son without sin but no Son without a cross. As Christians, we can be assured that we will have trials. But our confidence is that we will have victory over them through the presence of God. Psalm 23 says, "Yea, though I walk through the valley of the shadow of death, I will fear no evil; for thou art with me" (v. 4). Trials will come, but God's grace will meet us in our times of need. Trials come for several purposes.

Lesson

I. TRIALS TEST THE STRENGTH OF OUR FAITH

A. The Example of Hezekiah

There's a great illustration of how trials test the strength of one's faith in 2 Chronicles 32:31: "God left him [King Hezekiah], to test him, that he might know all that was in his heart." God didn't need to test Hezekiah to know what was in his heart. God already knew by omniscience. God tests us so we can find out. He assists us in doing a spiritual inventory on ourselves by bringing trials into our lives to demonstrate the strength or weakness of our faith. If you're currently experiencing a trial and are shaking your fist at God and wondering why it's happening, that's a good indication that you have weak faith. If, on the other hand, you're resting and rejoicing in the Lord, having placed the trial into His care, then you have strong faith.

B. The Example of Habakkuk

When Habakkuk was facing the threat of the Chaldeans coming and wiping out his people, he could still rejoice in the Lord: "Although the fig tree shall not blossom, neither shall fruit be in the vines; the labor of the olive shall fail, and the fields shall yield no food; the flock shall be cut off from the fold, and there shall be no herd in the stalls; yet I will rejoice in the Lord, I will joy in the God of my salvation. The Lord God is my strength, and he will make my feet like hinds' [mountain goats'] feet, and he will make me walk upon mine high places" (3:17-19). In the midst of the unsolvable mystery of why God allows the wicked to continue, the prophet recognized the sovereignty and wisdom of God and was thereby strengthened.

C. The Example of Job

As a result of his testing, Job admitted before God, "I have heard of thee by the hearing of the ear, but now mine eye seeth thee. Wherefore I abhor myself, and repent in

13

dust and ashes" (42:5-6). Job confessed his sin of questioning God's wisdom and sovereignty when the trials he experienced had exposed the weakness of his faith.

II. TRIALS HUMBLE US

Trials remind us not to think too highly of our spiritual strength. That is illustrated by the testimony of Paul in 2 Corinthians 12:7: "Lest I should be exalted above measure through the abundance of the revelations, there was given to me a thorn in the flesh." Paul had seen three visions of Jesus in His resurrection glory. Also, God had bestowed on him the power to do miracles and reveal truth. Such unique gifts could have led him to be proud. But God struck him with a painful, chronic problem that forced him to rely on Him.

Some people believe the "thorn" was malaria picked up from his travels or an eye disease alluded to in Galatians 4:15 and 6:11. Other people believe it was demonic opposition that was continually besetting him because he identified it as "the messenger of Satan to buffet me, lest I should be exalted above measure" (v. 7). Whatever it was, God used that trial to lead Paul to humbly depend on Him. God allows trials in our lives to keep us humble—especially when we are blessed to be in a position of spiritual service. They can prevent us from becoming over-confident of our spiritual strength.

III. TRIALS WEAN US FROM WORLDLY THINGS

A. Explained

The longer we live the more we accumulate—more furniture, cars, and investments—and we may experience more success or opportunities for travel. But in spite of the increase of worldly goods and pleasures, those things tend to be less and less significant in the lives of Christians. Perhaps you once believed such things were desirable, but now you realize they are incapable of solving the anxieties, hurts, and deeper problems of life. When trials come into your life and you reach out for those worldly things, you see what little lasting difference they make. Trials can wean you away from worldly things as

14

they demonstrate their utter inability to solve any problem or provide any resource in a time of stress.

B. Exemplified

1. By Jesus

In John 6 Jesus "lifted up his eyes, and saw a great company come unto him [and] saith unto Philip, Where shall we buy bread, that these may eat? And this he said to test him; for he himself knew what he would do" (vv. 5-6). Philip's response was from a worldly viewpoint, for he commented that he and the other disciples didn't have enough money to feed such a crowd (v. 7). Jesus wanted to find out whether Philip looked to worldly resources or to Him for the answer. Once the disciples' inability to meet the need had been established, Jesus went on to demonstrate His miraculous power and lifted them to greater faith in Him.

2. By Moses

Moses had been raised in Pharaoh's house as a prince of Egypt. As part of the royal family, he had the best education and reached the apex of Egyptian society in terms of wealth, honor, and comfort. But Hebrews 11:26 tells us that he considered the sacrifices made in identifying with God's purposes "greater riches than the treasures in Egypt." He took his eyes off all of the worldly things available to him and began to be concerned about the trials of his people, which the Lord used to wean him away from those passing pleasures.

IV. TRIALS CALL US TO AN ETERNAL HOPE

A. Stated

The flip side of the previous point is that trials in a believer's life increase his anticipation for heaven. Just as trials create a growing disinterest in the passing world, they also create a greater desire, for example, to be reunited with a loved one who has gone to be with the Lord. If the most precious people in your life have entered into the presence of God, and if you have invested your time and money in eternal things, then you won't have much tying you to this passing world.

B. Supported

1. Romans 8—Paul said, "The Spirit himself beareth witness with our spirit, that we are children of God; and if children, then heirs—heirs of God, and joint heirs with Christ—if so be that we suffer with him, that we may be also glorified together. For I reckon that the sufferings of this present time are not worthy to be compared with the glory which shall be revealed in us. For the earnest expectation of the creation waiteth for the manifestation of the sons of God. . . . The creation itself also shall be delivered from the bondage of corruption into the glorious liberty of the children of God. For we know that the whole creation groaneth and travaileth in pain together until now. . . . We ourselves groan within ourselves, waiting for the adoption, that is, the redemption of our body, for we are saved by hope" (vv. 16-19, 21-24). Beyond this life of suffering is a glorious future for the believer that makes us all the more desirous for the fulfillment of salvation.

2. 2 Corinthians 4—Paul said, "We faint not; but though our outward man perish, yet the inward man is renewed day by day. For our light affliction, which is but for a moment, worketh for us a far more exceeding and eternal weight of glory, while we look not at the things which are seen, but at the things which are not seen; for the things which are seen are temporal, but the things which are not seen are eternal" (vv. 16-18). Trials give us a greater affection for that which is eternal. They help us long for the eternal city of heaven.

    You may wonder how Paul acquired that kind of attitude. In verses 8-10 he says, "We are troubled on every side . . . we are perplexed . . . persecuted . . . cast down . . . always bearing about in the body the dying of the Lord Jesus." Paul was going through so much trouble, it's little wonder he didn't like the world and preferred to be in glory.

V. TRIALS REVEAL WHAT WE REALLY LOVE

A. Stated

Apart from God, nothing could have been dearer to Abraham than his son Isaac. But that was the test: to find out whether he loved Isaac more than God. Trials test our love for God by how we react to them. If we love God supremely, we will thank God for what He is accomplishing through our trials. But if we love ourselves more than God, we will question God's wisdom and become upset and bitter. If anything is dearer to us than God, then He must remove it in order for us to grow spiritually.

B. Supported

1. Deuteronomy 13:3—Moses warned the Israelites about following false prophets, saying, "Thou shalt not hearken to the words of that prophet, or that dreamer of dreams; for the Lord your God testeth you, to know whether ye love the Lord your God with all your heart and with all your soul." The Lord tests us to see if we truly love Him as much as we claim.

2. Luke 14:26-27—Jesus said, "If any man come to me, and hate not his father, and mother, and wife, and children, and brethren, and sisters, yea, and his own life also, he cannot be my disciple. And whosoever doth not bear his cross, and come after me, cannot be my disciple." Jesus was not saying we're to hate everyone. Rather He meant that if you do not love God to the degree that you willingly, if necessary, cut yourself off from your father, mother, spouse, children, brother, sister, or even your own life, then you don't love Him supremely. You must determine to do the will of God first and foremost, no matter what appeals others may make to you. In Jewish thinking, this devotion to God would be so intense that devotion to one's family would seem like hatred in comparison. In the case of Abraham, in Genesis 22 we see who he loved most. Abraham loved God more than his only son.

VI. TRIALS TEACH US TO VALUE GOD'S BLESSINGS

A. Explained

The world tells us that life is just the here and now, so we should enjoy it at any price. But faith tells us to value God's Word, obey it, and receive His blessing. Trials teach us the blessings of obedience. When we obey God's will in the midst of a trial, we are blessed.

B. Exemplified

1. By David

In Psalm 63:3 David says, "Because thy loving-kindness is better than life, my lips shall praise thee." That was written in the context of King Saul's mad pursuit to kill David (1 Sam. 23:14). Certainly trials like that enabled David to experience God's loving-kindness as he trusted in His protection.

2. By Jesus

Jesus is the perfect example of one who was blessed for His obedience. Hebrews 5:7-9 says that "in the days of his flesh, when he had offered up prayers and supplications with strong crying and tears unto him that was able to save him from death, and was heard in that he feared, though he were a Son, yet learned he obedience by the things which he suffered; and being made perfect, he became the author of eternal salvation to all them that obey him." That is a reference to Jesus' suffering in the Garden of Gethsemane (Luke 22:39-44). He chose to obey the Father's will, saying, "Not my will, but thine, be done" (v. 42). Philippians 2:8-9 mentions the results of His obedience: "He humbled himself and became obedient unto death, even the death of the cross. Wherefore, God also hath highly exalted him."

Trials put us through suffering so that we might obey and then receive the full blessing of God. As you learn to obey God, you will experience the exhilaration of that blessing.

VII. TRIALS ENABLE US TO HELP OTHERS IN THEIR SUFFERING

A. The Exhortation

Sometimes when suffering comes, it may have no more purpose than to make us better able to assist others in their own suffering. In Luke 22:31-32 Jesus says to Peter, "Simon, Simon, behold, Satan hath desired to have you, that he may sift you as wheat. But I have prayed for thee, that thy faith fail not. And when thou art converted [restored], strengthen thy brethren."

All Christians have a responsibility to help those who are suffering. Second Corinthians 1:3-4 tells us that we go through trials for the purpose of comforting others with the comfort we have received. It is wonderful that God allows us to learn by experience to instruct others.

B. The Example

Hebrews 4:13-16 tells us Jesus is able to help all who come to Him because He has been through every trial we've been through. That's what makes Him a merciful high priest.

VIII. TRIALS PRODUCE ENDURANCE AND STRENGTH

Thomas Manton said that while all things are quiet and comfortable, we live by sense rather than faith. But the worth of a soldier is never known in times of peace. One of God's purposes in trials is to give us greater strength. As you go through one trial, your spiritual muscles (faith) are exercised and strengthened for the next one. That means you can face greater foes and endure greater obstacles, thus becoming more useful to the Lord. And the more useful you are, the more you will accomplish His will in the power of His Spirit for His glory.

Focusing on the Facts

1. What made God's request of Abraham in Genesis 22:2 so difficult (see p. 9)?
2. Describe Abraham's response to God's request (see p. 10).
3. What was Abraham's test designed to show (see p. 11)?
4. Like Abraham, what must we be willing to give up (see p. 11)?
5. What enabled Abraham to pass such a test? Explain (Heb. 11:17; see pp. 11-12).
6. What does the account of Abraham tell us about what a man can do when facing the severest trial (see p. 12)?
7. Can Christians expect a perfect environment of comfort? Explain. What should be our confidence (see p. 12)?
8. Since God knows what's in our hearts, why does He test us (see p. 13)?
9. If a person is facing a trial, what response will indicate that he has weak faith? What response indicates that he has strong faith (see p. 13)?
10. Explain the purpose of Paul's "thorn in the flesh" (2 Cor. 12:7; see p. 14).
11. What perspective did Moses have that allowed him to forfeit the treasures of Egypt (Heb. 11:26; see p. 15)?
12. If you have invested your time and money in eternal things, what kind of relationship will you have with the passing world (see p. 16)?
13. Why was Paul not defeated by the suffering he endured (Rom. 8:18-24; 2 Cor. 4:16-18; see p. 16)?
14. What did Jesus mean by saying that His followers must hate their families (Luke 14:26-27; see p. 17)?
15. What does the world tell us to value? What does faith tell us to value (see p. 18)?
16. What blessings resulted from Jesus' obedience to do the Father's will (Heb. 5:7-9; Phil. 2:8-9; see p. 18)?
17. Explain how trials can result in our greater usefulness to the Lord (see p. 19).

Pondering the Principles

1. It is a natural tendency for people to reach out to worldly goods and pleasures for security, comfort, or meaning in the midst of difficult circumstances. Psalm 20:6-8 says, "Now I know that

the Lord saves His anointed; He will answer him from His holy heaven, with the saving strength of His right hand. Some boast in chariots, and some in horses; but we will boast in the name of the Lord, our God. They have bowed down and fallen; but we have risen and stood upright" (NASB). When you face a crisis, what resource do you turn to—the Word or the world? Meditate on Psalm 34, praising the One who is "near to the brokenhearted" and who rescues the righteous from their afflictions (vv. 18-19).

2. One purpose of trials is that they enable us to help others in their suffering. Read 2 Corinthians 1:3-11. Think about how you have been comforted by the "God of all comfort" (v. 3). Now think of those in your midst who are going through trials you have faced before. Pray for opportunities to be a source of comfort and encouragement to others who, for example, have lost a loved one or have been laid off from work. Help direct their faith from themselves to "God, who raises the dead" (v. 9).

2
From Trouble to Triumph—Part 1

Outline

Introduction
A. The Reason for Trials
B. The Result of Trials
1. Happiness
2. Endurance
   a) The proof of faith
     (1) 1 John 4:19
     (2) 1 John 2:15
     (3) 1 Peter 1:6-8
   b) The perseverance of the saints
     (1) Divine sovereignty
       (*a*) The promise and power of God
       (*b*) The prayers of Christ
       (*c*) The presence of the Holy Spirit
     (2) Human responsibility
       (*a*) Stated
       (*b*) Supported
       (*c*) Shunned
       (*d*) Summarized
C. The Reward of Trials
1. 2 Timothy 4:8
2. 1 Peter 5:4
3. Revelation 2:10

Introduction

The subject of trials is a natural starting point for the simple reason that everyone in the world encounters them. Because we are sinful

23

beings who live in a fallen world, we experience trouble on a regular basis whether we are Christians or not. Even when we succeed in getting our own little worlds under control, something inevitably messes them up. We do everything we can to attain peace and comfort by protecting ourselves from trouble, but trouble arises nonetheless. Marriage was designed as a source of fulfillment and happiness, yet 1 Corinthians 7:28 says those who are married "shall have trouble in the flesh." There is going to be trouble even in the best of what God gives to us because of the sin principle that is active in the world.

Jesus Himself experienced trouble and warned His disciples to expect tribulation in the world (John 16:33). John 11:33, 12:27, and 13:21 record Jesus' troubled responses to the devastating effects of sin.

Paul said he was "troubled on every side" (2 Cor. 4:8). It is reasonable to expect trouble in our lives as well. We experience trouble in our families, from our friends, on our jobs, at school, and with our nation. It comes in the form of criticism, persecution, illness, death of loved ones, personality conflicts, or inflation. Trouble is a way of life, so don't think you're alone if you're experiencing it.

A. The Reason for Trials

Jewelers use "the water test" as one of the surest ways to identify a true diamond. An imitation stone is never as brilliant as a genuine stone, but sometimes the difference can't be determined with the unaided eye. Jewelers know that a genuine diamond placed in water sparkles brilliantly, whereas the sparkle of the imitation is practically extinguished. That test makes picking the real diamond relatively easy.

By way of analogy I find that the faith of many people under the water of sorrow or affliction is nothing but an imitation. However, when a true child of God is immersed in a trial, he will shine as brilliantly as ever.

Early twentieth-century scholar G. K. Chesterton stated the same idea in a similar way: "I believe in getting into hot water. I think it keeps you clean." There is, to be sure, the need for testing to see if we are genuine believers. Some-

24

times there is no better test than the hot water of difficult circumstances. How one handles trouble is an indication of the reality of one's faith or the lack of it. That is why James, whose purpose is to give us tests of living faith, introduces the test of trials.

James says that if my Christianity is genuine, it will prove itself in times of trouble. If my faith in God is only good when I'm doing well, then it is of little value. True faith is to sustain me when everything goes wrong. James 1:2 says, "My brethren, count it all joy when ye fall into various trials." The Greek word translated "various" (*poikilos*) means "many colored" or "variegated." It emphasizes not the number but the diversity of trouble that can come our way. The Greek word translated "trials" (*peirasmos*) refers to that which breaks the pattern of tranquillity or happiness. We don't know what specific trials James had in mind as he wrote, but his instruction is applicable to any trial we might encounter.

Trial or Temptation?

Peirasmos is not necessarily connected with evil. It's unfortunate that the King James Version has translated it as "temptation," because of the evil connotation that word carries. So a trial is not necessarily a solicitation to do evil, as the context here clearly shows. Rather, in verse 2 "trials" refers to the difficulties God allows for the proving and strengthening of our faith.

Peirasmos is rare in secular Greek but common in biblical Greek because the testing of faith is such an important part of spiritual life. The verb form means "to put someone to the test," regardless of whether the results of the testing are positive or negative. Every trial that comes into your life becomes a test of your faith. You either pass or fail. To fail the test by wrongly responding to it allows it to become a temptation. If it ends up leading you to stumble, it has proved to be successful in tempting you. If it ends up in victory, it has proved to be successful in strengthening you. How you respond to the trials in your life will reveal whether you really believe God and are genuinely saved, and it will also reveal how strong your faith really is.

James is not distinguishing here between internal and external trials because that's an artificial distinction. I have found in my life that every external trial soon becomes internal. No trial I've ever seen stays on the outside; otherwise it isn't much of a trial. It's when it gets in and festers in my mind that it becomes a trial. Any trial is external and internal.

Trials come in the form of disappointments, frustrations, misunderstandings, unfulfilled dreams, unmet expectations, great loss, loneliness, fear, criticism, persecution, and conflict. Although they may start on the outside, sooner or later they end up on the inside.

Trials come for the purpose of testing our faith and therefore apply to believers as well as unbelievers. If you consistently persevere through trials and never abandon your trust in God, then you prove to have genuine faith.

Robert Johnstone, writing in a commentary on James many years ago, said, "[James shows that] where there is but an empty profession, or a mere dreamy sentiment, unbased on firm and intelligent convictions of truth, the fire of trouble will burn it up. . . . But where there is true faith, affliction naturally leads to deeper thought than under other circumstances on sin and its deserts, and thus frees the heart from the control of self-righteousness. The sense of weakness leads to earnest wrestling with God in prayer; and experience of the sustaining grace thus obtained strengthens and exhilarates hope with regard to the time to come" (*Lectures Exegetical and Practical on the Epistle of James* [Minneapolis: Klock & Klock, 1978 reprint], p. 74). When a false Christian goes through a test, it will inevitably reveal his true colors. When a true believer goes through a test, he will be driven to prayer, leaning on the strength of God rather than his own weakness. Trials burn up imitation faith but strengthen true faith. They may cause us pain when we are confronted with our weaknesses, but they have the good result of causing us to turn from ourselves to the infinite strength of God.

B. The Result of Trials

1. Happiness

James ends his discourse on trials in verse 12: "Blessed is the man that endureth temptation [trials]; for when he is tried [after his trial is over], he shall receive the crown of life, which the Lord hath promised to them that love him." James 5:11 reiterates the same thought: "Behold, we count them happy who endure." People who successfully endure trials are truly happy.

James is not saying happiness comes in freedom from trials but in victory over them. There is a big difference. It's not the shallow joy of the spectator who never experienced conflict; it's the exuberance of the participant who fought and won. James here is not referring to temptation. If that were the case, he wouldn't have said happy is the man who endures it, but happy is the man who resists it.

Since the three key ideas in verse 12 are endurance, trials, and being tested, and the same ideas appear in verses 2-3, it is easy to conclude that the testing of our faith through trials is the theme of verses 2-12.

2. Endurance

Endurance in verse 12 speaks of patiently and triumphantly enduring. It connotes passive or even painful survival and focuses on the outcome of being victorious. The person who goes through trials and comes out a winner never gives up his faith or abandons God. He is shown to be genuine, and all genuine Christians will receive the crown of life.

Some people come to the church, profess Christ, and even get baptized. Yet when trouble comes into their lives, they're gone. And they may never come back. Maybe they encountered a broken relationship, the death of a loved one, or some other struggle, and the circumstances were so overpowering that they blamed

God and walked away, convinced that Christianity doesn't work.

a) The proof of faith

Persevering through trials is proof of living faith. James identifies those who persevere as people who love God (v. 12). That's because loving God is the natural outflow of salvation.

(1) 1 John 4:19—John said, "We love him [God], because he first loved us." Christianity is a love relationship between man and God. Salvation is not a transaction whereby God grants us eternal life no matter what our attitude is toward Him. Those who are truly saved have a deep ongoing love for God.

(2) 1 John 2:15—John said, "If any man love the world, the love of the Father is not in him." People will love God or the world, but not both. Unbelievers who profess Christ demonstrate that they love the world when they depart from the truth. It's in the trial that true love is made manifest. First John 2:19 says, "They went out from us, but they were not of us; for if they had been of us, they would no doubt have continued with us; but they went out, that they might be made manifest they were not all of us."

(3) 1 Peter 1:6-8—Peter said, "In this ye greatly rejoice, though now for a season, if need be, ye are in heaviness through manifold trials, that the trial of your faith, being much more precious than of gold that perisheth, though it be tried with fire, might be found unto praise and honor and glory at the appearing of Jesus Christ, whom, having not seen, ye love." Our faith is being tested to prove its genuineness so we will be able to stand before the Lord with genuine faith when He comes.

A Christian is not someone who simply at one point in time believed the truth. A true believer has an ongoing love for God that holds fast even in trials. Jesus said several times that a person who loves Him will keep His commandments (John 14:15, 23; 15:9-10; 1 John 2:5-6; 5:1-3). The genuineness of faith is built on love that obeys God.

As believers we may experience times of struggle and doubt, but our faith will never be destroyed. We cling to the Lord despite our trials because we love Him. That kind of loving perseverance results in true blessing.

One purpose of testing is to expose the quality of our faith. The phrase "for when he is tried" in verse 12 can be translated "when he is approved after testing." When tests come into your life in the form of loneliness, a death, or a financial loss, God is putting you through the fire, as it were, that you might come out with the dross burned off and your true faith shining bright. Those who hold fast to their trust in God through trials show that their faith is living.

b) The perseverance of the saints

The important biblical truth known as the perseverance of the saints is a major tenet of Reformed Protestant theology. We believe that the saints will never abandon their faith; they will always persevere in believing God through every trial until they are glorified. True believers won't believe for a little while and then bail out. That is evident from 1 Corinthians 10:13: "There hath no temptation [trial] taken you but such as is common to man; but God is faithful, who will not permit you to be tempted above that ye are able, but will, with the temptation, also make the way to escape, that ye may be able to bear it."

I grew up hearing the phrases "eternal security" and "once saved, always saved." Those are accurate descriptions of what Scripture teaches. The Bible doesn't say, "Once saved, but you never know for how long." Some people wrongfully conclude, however, that eternal security implies you can do anything you want if you're saved, as if God were stuck

with you and there were no disciplinary consequences for sin. They emphasize the sovereign power of God and His unchanging promise in securing
our salvation but to the exclusion of how a person
who has been spiritually reborn is responsible to live.

(1) Divine sovereignty

The Trinity secures us forever so that no Christian who believes in the Lord will ever be lost.
Scripture bases the eternal security of the believer
on:

(a) The promise and power of God

Our eternal security is based on the covenant-
al faithfulness of God. He preserves His people from apostasy and brings them all to heav-
en.

i) Psalm 31:24—"Be of good courage, and he
[God] shall strengthen your heart, all ye
that hope in the Lord."

ii) Psalm 37:23, 28—"The steps of a good
man are ordered by the Lord. . . . The
Lord loveth justice, and forsaketh not his
saints; they are preserved forever."

iii) Psalm 97:10—"Ye who love the Lord, hate
evil. He preserveth the souls of his saints;
he delivereth them out of the hand of the
wicked."

iv) Psalm 121:4-7—"Behold, he who keepeth
Israel shall neither slumber nor sleep. The
Lord is thy keeper; the Lord is thy shade
upon thy right hand. The sun shall not
smite thee by day, nor the moon by night.
The Lord shall preserve thee from all evil;
he shall preserve thy soul."

v) John 6:37, 39—Jesus said, "All that the Father giveth me shall come to me . . . of all that he hath given me I should lose nothing."

vi) John 10:28-29—Jesus said, "I give unto them [those who follow Christ] eternal life; and they shall never perish, neither shall any man pluck them out of my hand. My Father, who gave them to me, is greater than all, and no man is able to pluck them out of my Father's hand."

vii) Romans 16:25—Paul said, "Now to him that is of power to establish you according to my gospel."

viii) Philippians 1:6—"He who hath begun a good work in you will perform it until the day of Jesus Christ."

ix) 1 Thessalonians 5:23-24—Paul said, "The very God of peace sanctify you wholly; and I pray God your whole spirit and soul and body be preserved blameless unto the coming of our Lord Jesus Christ. Faithful is he that calleth you, who also will do it."

x) 2 Timothy 1:12—Paul said, "I know whom I have believed and am persuaded that he is able to keep that which I have committed unto him against that day." He had committed his soul to God.

xi) 2 Timothy 4:18—Paul said, "The Lord shall deliver me from every evil work, and will preserve me unto his heavenly kingdom."

xii) 1 Peter 1:5—Christians "are kept by the power of God."

xiii) Jude 1—Christians are "preserved in Jesus Christ."

xiv) Jude 24—"Now unto him that is able to keep you from falling, and to present you faultless before the presence of his glory with exceeding joy."

(b) The prayers of Christ

Christ constantly intercedes on our behalf as our Redeemer and Advocate so that any sin we commit does not alter the status of our salvation.

i) John 17:20-24—Jesus prayed for His present and future disciples to enter into the fullness of salvation.

ii) Luke 22:31-32—Jesus told Peter, "Satan hath desired to have you, that he may sift you as wheat; but I have prayed for thee, that thy faith fail not. And when thou art converted [recommitted after Christ's resurrection] strengthen thy brethren."

iii) 1 John 2:1-2—John said, "If any man sin, we have an advocate with the Father, Jesus Christ the righteous; and he is the propitiation for our sins, and not for ours only, but also for the sins of the whole world." Christ is our intercessor.

(c) The presence of the Holy Spirit

The indwelling Holy Spirit is our guarantee of future glory. Ephesians 1:13-14 says Christians have been "sealed with that Holy Spirit of promise, who is the earnest of our inheritance until the redemption of the purchased possession."

(2) Human responsibility

(*a*) Stated

There's another side to eternal security than just the predestinating work of God. It's the human perspective of the perseverance of believers. You reveal you are kept by God if you don't abandon your faith in the midst of a trial. The paradox of the sovereign work of God and the responsibility of man is common in Scripture. A believer is saved because he was chosen by God before creation (Eph. 1:4), yet he is not saved without exercising faith (Rom. 10:9-10). He is secure because of the covenant faithfulness of God, but he is still responsible to persevere. Eternal security is wrought through the power of the Spirit in energizing the true believer to endure all trials.

Theologian Louis Berkhof calls perseverance "that continuous operation of the Holy Spirit in the believer, by which the work of divine grace that is begun in the heart, is continued and brought to completion" (*Systematic Theology* [Grand Rapids: Eerdmans, 1941], p. 546). Our part is to endure.

(*b*) Supported

i) Matthew 24:13—"He that shall endure unto the end, the same shall be saved." That appears to contradict the fact that God is going to keep us saved, but it doesn't. We are energized to endure by the indwelling Spirit.

ii) John 8:31—"Then said Jesus to those Jews who believed on him, If ye continue in my word, then are ye my disciples indeed."

iii) 1 Corinthians 15:1-2—Paul said, "I declare unto you the gospel which I preached unto you, which also ye have received,

33

and in which ye stand; by which also ye are saved, if ye keep in memory what I preach unto you, unless ye have believed in vain." If you don't hold onto your faith, you show it wasn't real.

iv) Colossians 1:21-23—"You, that were once alienated and enemies in your mind by wicked works, yet now hath he reconciled in the body of his flesh through death, to present you holy and unblamable and unreprovable in his sight, if ye continue in the faith grounded and settled, and be not moved away from the hope of the gospel." You're secure only if you endure. Endurance is the process by which the security of one's salvation is verified.

v) Hebrews 2:1—"We ought to give the more earnest heed to the things which we have heard, lest any time we should let them slip."

vi) Hebrews 3:14—"We are made partakers of Christ, if we hold the beginning of our confidence steadfast unto the end."

vii) Hebrews 4:14—"Let us hold fast our profession."

viii) Hebrews 6:11-12—"We desire that every one of you do show the same diligence to the full assurance of hope unto the end; that ye be not slothful, but followers of them who through faith and patience inherit the promises."

ix) Hebrews 10:39—"We are not of them who draw back unto perdition, but of them who believe to the saving of the soul."

x) 2 Peter 1:10—"Give diligence to make your calling and election sure; for if ye do these things, ye shall never fall."

(c) Shunned

When someone doesn't endure, he fails the test of genuine faith (1 John 2:19). No trial is so great that it could sever you from your Lord if your faith is genuine (1 Cor. 10:13). Eternal security is not a matter of being once saved, always saved—with no regard for what you believe or do. Hebrews 12:14 says only those who continue living holy lives will enter the Lord's presence.

The contemporary trend labeled "easy believism" holds that only a decision to accept Christ is necessary to be born again, regardless of one's sincerity. But if a person fails to love and obey the Lord through the trials of life, then there is no evidence that he possesses saving faith. How many people do you know who came to church for a while, had a little trouble in their lives, and left? Although they may have made a profession of faith in Christ, they cannot be identified as those who love Him because their lives are not characterized by an enduring obedience.

(d) Summarized

Here's what the Westminster Confession of Faith says about the perseverance of the saints: "They whom God hath accepted in his Beloved, effectually called and sanctified by his Spirit, can neither totally nor finally fall away from the state of grace; but shall certainly persevere therein to the end and be eternally saved. This perseverance of the saints depends, not upon their own free-will, but on the immutability of the decree of election, flowing from the free and unchangeable love of God the Father; upon the efficacy of the merit and intercession of Jesus Christ; the abiding of the Spirit and of the seed of God within them; and the nature of the covenant of grace: from all which ariseth also the certainty and infallibility thereof. Nevertheless they may, through the temptations of Satan and of the world, the prevalence of corruption remaining in them, and the neglect of the means of their preservation, fall into grievous sins; and for a time continue therein: whereby they incur God's displeasure, and grieve his Holy Spirit; come to be deprived of some measure of their graces and comforts; have their hearts hardened, their consciences wounded; hurt and scandalize others, and bring temporal judgments upon themselves" (Philip Schaff, ed., *The Creeds of Christendom*, vol. 3 [Grand Rapids: Baker, 1977], pp. 636-37).

A Christian may get himself into trouble, but he will never ultimately discard his faith because he will persevere. Whenever trials come into our lives, they prove the genuineness of our faith by giving us the opportunity to persevere. And having persevered, a believer can look back and say, "Yes, I know I belong to the Lord."

C. The Reward of Trials

The reward for the believer who does not collapse under trials is eternal life. James says, "When he is tried [approved], he shall receive the crown of life" (1:12). The "crown of life" is an appositional genitive in the Greek text, which means it could literally be translated "a crown which is life." The crown is eternal life, which God has promised to those who love Him. That is the believer's ultimate reward. Although we presently experience some of the benefits of eternal life, we possess it on promise; some day we're going to receive it in its fullness. We are still waiting to enter into our future reward. At the Lord's coming, He will grant to us the fullness of eternal life.

1. 2 Timothy 4:8—The apostle Paul expressed a similar thought: "Henceforth there is laid up for me a crown of righteousness, which the Lord, the righteous judge, shall give me at that day; and not to me only, but to all them also that love his appearing." When Christ returns for the church, Christians will be granted a life of eternal righteousness.

2. 1 Peter 5:4—"When the chief shepherd shall appear, ye shall receive a crown of glory."

3. Revelation 2:10—Christ promised the crown of life to the Christians of Smyrna if they remained faithful until death.

We will all receive the same crown consisting of the rewards of eternal life, righteousness, and glory. Endurance does not earn eternal life. However, endurance is the proof of true faith and love, and that is rewarded by eternal life. That's an important distinction.

The Greek word translated "crown" in James 1:12 is *stephanos*. In the ancient Greek world, it often referred to the wreath put around the head of a victor in an athletic event. The Lord will reward with eternal life those who demonstrate with the perseverance of an athlete that they were truly saved.

How Can a Christian Endure Trials?

James 1 tells us several things are required:

1. A joyous attitude—"Count it all joy" (v. 2). That prevents you from avoiding trials the Lord intends you to face and provides the motivation to face them head on.

2. An understanding mind—"Knowing this" (v. 3). That allows you to perceive the reality and purpose of a trial.

3. A submissive will—"Let patience have her perfect work" (v. 4). That allows you to accept it from the Lord and learn what He wants you to learn.

4. A believing heart—"Let him ask in faith, nothing wavering. . . . A double minded man is unstable" (vv. 6-8). That allows you to remain firm in spite of difficult circumstances.

5. A humble spirit—"The brother of low degree is exalted . . . but the rich . . . shall pass away" (vv. 9-11). That allows you to accept God's greater wisdom, recognizing that what is valuable in life is eternal.

Focusing on the Facts

1. Why do people experience trouble on a regular basis (see pp. 23-24)?
2. Explain how the water test a jeweler uses is analogous to the testing God puts us through (see p. 24).
3. What do trials reveal in a person (see p. 25)?
4. Are trials necessarily connected with evil? Explain their relationship to temptation (see p. 25).
5. Although trials may cause pain in confronting us with our weaknesses, what positive result can come about from facing them (see p. 26)?
6. What does James 1:12 say are two results of trials (p. 27)?
7. Is James saying that happiness comes in freedom from trials? Explain (see p. 27).
8. Whom does James identify as those who persevere (v. 12; see p. 28)?
9. What will true faith in God manifest itself in, according to John 14:15 and 1 John 5:1-3 (see pp. 28-29)?
10. Describe the doctrine of the perseverance of the saints (see p. 29).
11. What do some people wrongfully conclude about the doctrine of perseverance (see pp. 29-30)?
12. What are three reasons for believing that Christians are eternally secure? Support your answer with Scripture (see pp. 30-32).
13. Identify and explain the aspect besides divine sovereignty that relates to the believer's endurance. Support your answer with Scripture (see pp. 33-35).
14. When a person professing to be a Christian fails to endure, what does he reveal (1 John 2:19; see p. 35)?
15. Describe the contemporary trend regarding accepting Christ and obedience (see p. 35).

16. Identify the results of true believers falling into "grievous sins," as explained in the Westminster Confession of Faith (see p. 36).
17. What is the reward of remaining faithful through trials (see p. 36)?
18. Does endurance earn eternal life? Explain (see p. 37).

Pondering the Principles

1. Have you passed the test of trials? Did they reveal a continuing love for God or a passing sense of religious duty? Can you look back and see your trust in God's faithfulness and wisdom growing stronger? Memorize 1 Corinthians 10:13: "No temptation has overtaken you but such as is common to man; and God is faithful, who will not allow you to be tempted beyond what you are able, but with the temptation will provide the way of escape also, that you may be able to endure it" (NASB*).

2. How are you responding to trials? Reread the quote from Robert Johnstone on page 26. Are your trials leading you to consider what God is doing in your life? Are you coming to God in prayer and experiencing His sustaining grace? Recall the trial Jesus experienced in the Garden of Gethsemane on the night of His arrest (Luke 22:39-46). In the trials you have recently experienced, were you able to say, "Not my will, but thine, be done" (v. 42)? Commit yourself to praying earnestly and seeking the Lord's will as you encounter your next trial.

3. Meditate on the apostle Paul's words in Romans 8:35-39: "What shall separate us from the love of Christ? Shall tribulation, or distress, or persecution, or famine, or nakedness, or peril, or sword? As it is written, For thy sake we are killed all the day long; we are accounted as sheep for the slaughter. Nay, in all these things we are more than conquerors through him that loved us. For I am persuaded that neither death, nor life, nor angels, nor principalities, nor powers, nor things present, nor things to come, nor height, nor depth, nor any other creation, shall be able to separate us from the love of God, which is in Christ Jesus, our Lord." No trial can ever sever us from the Lord. Praise the Lord for that great promise.

New American Standard Bible.

3
From Trouble to Triumph—Part 2

Outline

Review

Lesson
I. A Joyous Attitude (v. 2)
   A. Explained
   B. Expressed
      1. Hebrews 12:2
      2. Hebrews 12:11
      3. John 16:2, 20-22
   C. Exemplified
      1. By Jesus
      2. By Paul
      3. By Job
         a) Job 13:15
         b) Job 23:10
   D. Evaluated
II. An Understanding Mind (v. 3)
   A. Know the Reality of Testing
   B. Know the Reason for Testing
      1. Psalm 40:1-3
      2. 1 Corinthians 10:13
      3. 2 Thessalonians 1:2-4
   C. Know the Reward of Testing
      1. Hebrews 11:24-29
      2. Hebrews 11:32-39
III. A Submissive Will (v. 4)
   A. The Request for Submission (v. 4a)
      1. Psalm 131:1-3
      2. Job 5:7-11

      3. Psalm 37:1, 5

      4. 1 Peter 2:20

B. The Result of Submission (v. 4*b*)

Review

Loving God is without question the key to enduring all the trials of life. Perhaps it is the most decisive evidence of a regenerate soul. True Christians are designated by James as those who love God (1:12). They endure trials because they have a strong love for God. Any relationship where the bond of love is strong will endure all kinds of adversity. He who endures the trials of life will be rewarded, having revealed himself as one who really loves the Lord.

As Christians we are eternally secure not only from God's viewpoint but also as we persevere from our viewpoint. The perseverance of the saints describes those who hold fast to their love for God and their faith in Him. The question we will be answering in our study is this: How can we persevere through trials and be victorious in them? There are five keys to persevering through trials.

Lesson

I. A JOYOUS ATTITUDE (v. 2)

"My brethren, count it all joy when ye fall into various trials."

A. Explained

James addressed Jewish Christians, whom he identifies in verses 1-2 as brethren belonging to the twelve scattered tribes of Israel. He encouraged them to persevere through their various trials with a joyous attitude.

The Greek word translated "count" could also be translated "consider" or "evaluate." Evaluating a trial as being joyful is something a Christian must discipline himself to do, because joy is not the natural human response to troubles. He must make a conscious commitment to face each trial with a joyous attitude. Paul was a prisoner in Rome when he said to the Philippians, "Rejoice in the Lord always; and again I say, Rejoice. . . . I have learned, in whatever state I am, in this to be content" (4:4, 11). He had learned to be content and rejoice in the midst of trials. That's not something that happens by accident.

The Greek word translated "when," used in the subjunctive mood, means "whenever," implying the inevitability of trials. The compound Greek verb for "fall" (*peripipto*) literally means "to fall into the midst of." It is used in Luke 10:30 of the man the Good Samaritan found who fell among thieves. Acts 27:41 says the ship Paul was on fell "into a place where two seas met," a place of turbulence. The word conveys the idea of an unplanned, inadvertent occurrence that surrounds you. All of us are going to fall into the midst of inadvertent troubles from which there seems to be no clear way out.

B. Expressed

    1. Hebrews 12:2—Jesus never sought troubles, but He always accepted them. It was "for the joy that was set before him [that he] endured the cross, despising the shame." He went through the humiliation and suffering of crucifixion because He joyfully looked beyond the trial to what it would accomplish.

    2. Hebrews 12:11—"No chastening for the present seemeth to be joyous, but grievous; nevertheless, afterward it yieldeth the peaceable fruit of righteousness unto them who are exercised by it." When you see a trial coming, have an attitude of joy from anticipating the perfecting work the Lord will do through that trial. Learn to cultivate a right attitude.

Guaranteed Opportunities for Expressing Joy

Since the Lord went through pain to experience joy, we shouldn't expect anything different. Jesus told His disciples as He was preparing to send them out that they shouldn't expect anything different from what He had experienced. He said, "It is enough for the disciple that he be like his teacher" (Matt. 10:25, cf. John 13:16). Jesus was not talking about discipleship as modeling godliness but as

43

suffering. In John 15:18, 20 Jesus says, "If the world hate you, ye know that it hated me before it hated you. . . . If they have persecuted me, they will also persecute you." Trials are something every Christian can count on. But they are also new opportunities for joyful dependence on the One who allows them.

3. John 16:2, 20-22—Jesus warned His disciples, "The time cometh, that whosoever killeth you will think that he doeth God service. . . . Verily, verily, I say unto you, Ye shall weep and lament, but the world shall rejoice; and ye shall be sorrowful, but your sorrow shall be turned into joy. A woman, when she is in travail, hath sorrow, because her hour is come; but as soon as she is delivered of the child, she remembereth no more the anguish, for joy that a man is born into the world. And ye now, therefore, have sorrow; but I will see you again, and your heart shall rejoice, and your joy no man taketh from you." Similarly we can rejoice in seeing beyond to the greater outcome.

We must have a decisive conviction that we're going to face trials with a joyful attitude. It is the joy of one who counts it a privilege to have his faith tested because he knows the testing will draw him closer to the Savior. That is when a trial becomes a welcome friend.

In trials you are much more sensitive to the presence of God. Your communion with Him increases as you search the Scriptures to find answers to your problems and ask people to pray for you. That draws you closer to the Lord, the very source of your joy.

C. Exemplified

1. By Jesus

We have not yet suffered to the degree Jesus did (Heb. 12:4). Have you ever thought about that? When I'm going through a trial, I'm always reminded of that fact. If He could endure the cross and see it as a joyous opportunity to accomplish the purpose of God, then I should be able to endure my small trial with joy.

2. By Paul

The apostle Paul seems as close to being like Christ as any man will ever be. Whenever he encountered trials he responded by rejoicing.

a) Acts 16:25—On their second missionary journey Paul and Silas were thrown into jail. And it wouldn't have been a jail like those of today. Jails then were dark and filthy. The prisoners were often put in stocks, their limbs stretched to an extreme, which caused their muscles to tighten up into knots. Verse 25 says that, in spite of such circumstances, "at midnight Paul and Silas prayed, and sang praises unto God." That is a joyous attitude in the midst of a difficult trial.

b) 2 Corinthians 12:7-9—Paul mentioned "a thorn in the flesh, the messenger of Satan" that had caused him to suffer. Although he prayed three times for the Lord to remove that particular trial, it didn't go away. The Lord said to him, "My grace is sufficient for thee; for my strength is made perfect in weakness" (v. 9). Paul responded, "Most gladly, therefore, will I rather glory in my infirmities, that the power of Christ may rest upon me" (v. 9). Paul recognized that he didn't need the elimination of the trial—only the grace to endure it. He saw trials as something to draw him closer to the Lord (Phil. 3:10) and keep him humbly dependent on God's strength (2 Cor. 12:7-9).

c) Philippians 1:13-16, 18—Not all suffering is necessarily physical. Sometimes we go through emotional and mental suffering. Paul was a prisoner in Rome when he wrote to the Philippians. His ministry had been greatly curtailed. Nevertheless, he told the Philippians that his imprisonment had actually aided the furtherance of the gospel. Being chained to Roman soldiers, he had the opportunity to win them to the Lord (v. 13). There was a revival of sorts taking place in Caesar's palace. Paul told the Philippians, "All the saints greet you, chiefly they that are of Caesar's household" (4:22). The soldiers didn't know what they had on their hands: they believed they had a prisoner, but in reality they had a self-appointed evangelist to whom they were a captive audience!

Paul said, "Many of the brethren in the Lord, becoming confident by my bonds, are much more bold to speak the word without fear. Some, indeed, preach Christ even of envy and strife . . . [and] of contention, not sincerely, supposing to add affliction to my bonds" (1:14-16). Some had assumed Paul was in prison because he had failed in his ministry and the Lord had set him aside. Nevertheless he recognized that "whether in pretense or in truth, Christ is preached; and in that I do rejoice, yea, and will rejoice" (v. 18). What a model of rejoicing in the midst of a potentially frustrating and discouraging situation!

d) Philippians 2:17—"If I have to be offered upon the sacrifice and service of your faith, I joy, and rejoice with you all." If Paul had to die in the process of leading the Philippians to salvation, he could still rejoice because he considered himself expendable for God's purposes (cf. Acts 20:24).

e) Philippians 3:5-8—Paul, realizing the sacrifices that were necessary in the pursuit of the greatest priority, said, "[I was] circumcised the eighth day, of the stock of Israel, of the tribe of Benjamin, an Hebrew of the Hebrews; as touching the law, a Pharisee; concerning zeal, persecuting the church; touching the righteousness which is in the law, blameless. But what things were gain to me, those I counted loss for Christ. Yea doubtless, and I count all things but loss for the excellency of the knowledge of Christ Jesus, my Lord; for whom I have suffered the loss of all things, and do count them but refuse, that I may win Christ."

f) Philippians 4:4—"Rejoice in the Lord always; and again I say, Rejoice."

g) Romans 8:18—"The sufferings of this present time are not worthy to be compared with the glory which shall be revealed in us." We can joyfully endure suffering in the present because of the glorious future promised us.

Paul learned to rejoice in difficult situations because he knew they would bring him closer to the Lord as he depended on His power to accomplish His purposes. Trials should be faced with a joyful attitude because they bring about proved faith, strengthen us, draw us into communion with God as we identify with Christ in His sufferings, and promise us better things to come.

3. By Job

   a) Job 13:15—"Though he slay me, yet will I trust in him." Obviously his wife, who advised him to give up hope, saying, "Curse God, and die" (2:9), knew nothing of approaching trials with the right attitude.

   b) Job 23:10—"He knoweth the way that I take; when he hath tested me, I shall come forth as gold." Job had hope in the final product.

D. Evaluated

Commentator Warren Wiersbe said, "Our values determine our evaluations. If we value comfort more than character, then trials will upset us. If we value the material and physical more than the spiritual, we will not be able to 'count it all joy.' If we live only for the present and forget the future, then trials will make us bitter, not better" (*Be Mature* [Wheaton, Ill.: Victor, 1978], p. 23).

If you can't rejoice in your trials, your values are wrong. You have not realized that God has a purpose in them. J. Oswald Sanders in his book *Spiritual Leadership* quotes early twentieth-century poet and missionary to India Amy Carmichael ([Chicago: Moody, 1980], pp. 171-72):

> Hast thou no scar?
> No hidden scar on foot, or side, or hand?
> I hear thee sung as mighty in the land,
> I hear them hail thy bright ascendant star:
>
> Hast thou no scar?

47

Hast thou no wound?
Yet, I was wounded by the archers, spent.
Leaned me against the tree to die, and rent
By ravening beasts that compassed me, I
    swooned:
Hast thou no wound?

No wound? No scar?
Yes, as the master shall the servant be,
And pierced are the feet that follow Me;
But thine are whole. Can he have followed
    far
Who has no wound? No scar?

We should count it a privilege and joy to bear in our bodies
the marks of Christ (Gal. 6:17).

II. AN UNDERSTANDING MIND (v. 3)

"Knowing this, that the testing of your faith worketh patience."

If you're going to go through a trial victoriously, you've got to
know a few things.

A. Know the Reality of Testing

The Greek word translated "knowing" (*ginōskō*, "to know
through experience") directs our attention to the mind.
Not only are you to have a joyful attitude in trials but also
an understanding mind that comes from personal experience. You need to know that your faith will be tested.
When you come out of a trial and still have your faith, it
confirms that you're really a believer. If you ask me how I
know I'm a Christian, I'll tell you it's because I love the
Lord and have gone through difficult situations with my
faith still intact.

B. Know the Reason for Testing

The Greek word translated "testing" (*dokimion*) means
"proof." The Greek verb for "worketh" means "to
achieve" or "to accomplish." Don't ever believe trials don't
accomplish something. They're designed to produce "pa-

tience" (Gk., *hupomonēn*), better translated "endurance" or "perseverance." It's the tenacity of spirit that holds on under pressure while waiting patiently on God to remove the trial at the appointed time and then reward us. Each trial strengthens us as we gain more endurance.

God builds us up in the same way that a runner gradually develops the ability to run long distance. He starts small and works up to his maximum capacity. God allows increasingly greater trials in our lives to increase our endurance for greater ministry and joy, for the more difficult the battle, the sweeter the victory. When you come out of a difficult trial, you can rejoice over God's delivering you. That proves Him to be trustworthy, and that strengthens your faith.

1. Psalm 40:1-3—David said, "I waited patiently for the Lord, and he inclined unto me, and heard my cry. He brought me up also out of an horrible pit, out of the miry clay, and set my feet upon a rock, and established my goings. And he hath put a new song in my mouth." Every time you come out of a trial you should be stronger.

2. 1 Corinthians 10:13—Paul said, "There hath no temptation [trial] taken you but such as is common to man; but God is faithful, who will not permit you to be tempted above that ye are able." Not everyone has the same ability to endure trials. A new Christian with limited knowledge and experience is not going to have the ability to endure the trials a mature Christian might undergo. This verse is God's promise that He will never put you through a trial you can't handle. The Lord will bring us trials to test and strengthen our faith, thus producing the necessary endurance to encounter greater trials. God faithfully works in our lives in a personal way to allow trials, unique to each individual, to take us to higher levels of spiritual maturity.

3. 2 Thessalonians 1:2-4—Paul wrote the Thessalonians, saying, "Grace unto you, and peace, from God, our Father, and the Lord Jesus Christ. We are bound to thank God always for you, brethren, as it is fitting, because your faith groweth exceedingly, and the love of every

one of you all toward each other aboundeth, so that we ourselves glory in you in the churches of God for your patience [endurance] and faith in all your persecutions and tribulations that ye endure." Learning how to endure trials brought the Thessalonians growing faith, abounding love, and a tremendous testimony.

C. Know the Reward of Testing

Christ, while enduring the cross, anticipated the salvation of the world that would come as a result, and His return to glory. Likewise, we need to know that what's going on in our lives is producing something beneficial.

1. Hebrews 11:24-29—"By faith Moses, when he was come to years, refused to be called the son of Pharaoh's daughter, choosing rather to suffer affliction with the people of God than to enjoy the pleasures of sin for a season, esteeming the reproach of Christ greater riches than the treasures in Egypt; for he had respect unto the recompense of the reward. By faith he forsook Egypt, not fearing the wrath of the king; for he endured, as seeing him who is invisible. Through faith he kept the passover, and the sprinkling of blood, lest he that destroyed the first-born should touch them. By faith they passed through the Red Sea as by dry land, which the Egyptians, attempting to do, were drowned." Moses lived in light of what endurance would bring about in the future.

2. Hebrews 11:32-39—Many other Old Testament believers endured great trials because of their faith in God. The writer of Hebrews said, "The time would fail me to tell of Gideon, and of Barak, and of Samson, and of Jephthah; of David also, and Samuel, and of the prophets, who, through faith, subdued kingdoms, wrought righteousness, obtained promises, stopped the mouths of lions, quenched the violence of fire, escaped the edge of the sword, out of weakness were made strong, became valiant in fight, turned to flight the armies of the aliens. Women received their dead raised to life again, and others were tortured, not accepting deliverance, that they might obtain a better resurrection: and others

had trial of cruel mockings and scourgings, yea, more-
over, of bonds and imprisonment; they were stoned,
they were sawn asunder, were tested, were slain with
the sword; they wandered about in sheepskins and
goatskins; being destitute, afflicted, tormented (of
whom the world was not worthy); they wandered in
deserts, and in mountains, and in dens and caves of the
earth. And these all, having received witness through
faith, received not the promise."

Those named and unnamed heroes of the faith trusted
God in the midst of unbelievable circumstances because
their eyes were focused on their future reward. Hebrews 12:1-2 therefore exhorts us to "lay aside every
weight, and the sin which doth so easily beset us, and
. . . run with patience the race that is set before us,
looking to Jesus, the author and finisher of our faith,
who for the joy that was set before him endured the
cross, despising the shame." Christ is the greatest example of enduring trials with joy.

III. A SUBMISSIVE WILL (v. 4)

A. The Request for Submission (v. 4a)

"But let patience have her perfect work."

This is a command demanding submission to God's purposes for the trial. Don't fight the trial and shake your fist
at God. Accept it. If you refuse to submit to God, you may
bring on yourself further chastening. Hebrews 12:5-7
warns, "My son, despise not thou the chastening of the
Lord, nor faint when thou art rebuked of him; for whom
the Lord loveth he chasteneth, and scourgeth every son
whom he receiveth. If ye endure chastening, God dealeth
with you as sons." If you fight against God's perfecting
work, the trials may become more difficult.

The only productive way out of a trial is through it. If God
wants you in a trial, there are no shortcuts you can take
that will accomplish His purpose. First Corinthians 10:13
tells us that God provides the way of escape from each trial
but only after enabling us to endure the trial.

The Greek word translated "perfect" (*teleion*) is used in secular sources to refer to animals that are full grown. We can take it to mean "spiritually mature" in this context. That noble purpose should motivate us not to resist, for trials are the tools of His perfecting work in our lives.

1. Psalm 131:1-3—David here exemplifies the right submissive attitude: "Lord, my heart is not haughty, nor mine eyes lofty; neither do I exercise myself in great matters, or in things too high for me. Surely I have behaved and quieted myself, like a child that is weaned of his mother; my soul is even like a weaned child." David likened his spiritual contentment to the child who has gone through the difficult weaning process and entered a new level of maturity.

2. Job 5:7-11—Job thanked God and willfully submitted to every trial the Lord gave him, even though his heart was sometimes confused. It wasn't the circumstances that bothered Job; it was that he couldn't seem to get an answer from God. Eliphaz instructed Job, saying, "Man is born unto trouble, as the sparks fly upward. I would seek unto God, and unto God would I commit my cause, who doeth great things and unsearchable, marvelous things without number; who giveth rain upon the earth, and sendeth waters upon the fields, to set up on high those that are low, that those who mourn may be exalted to safety." When you go through a trial, commit yourself to God.

3. Psalm 37:1, 5—David said, "Fret not thyself because of evil doers. . . . Commit thy way unto the Lord; trust also in him, and he shall bring it to pass."

4. 1 Peter 2:20—Peter said, "If, when ye do well and suffer for it, ye take it patiently, this is acceptable with God." That is because you're really suffering on His behalf.

B. The Result of Submission (v. 4*b*)

"That ye may be perfect and entire, lacking nothing."

Perfection, not endurance, is the goal of trials. Endurance is only the means to that end. When you go through a trial,

52

you are strengthened and acquire greater endurance, which will allow you to go through greater trials to bring about spiritual maturity. "Perfect" obviously doesn't mean sinlessness—that would contradict James 3:2—but the maturity of spiritual fathers who "have known him [God] that is from the beginning" (1 John 2:14). When our faith is tested we're driven to deeper communion and greater trust in our Lord. That produces the stability of godly character and righteous living. In Galatians 4:19 Paul says, "My little children, of whom I travail in birth again until Christ be formed in you." God's ultimate goal is for every believer to become like Christ.

James says that trials will make us "complete" (Gk., *holokleros; holos* means "whole" and *kleros* means "all the portions"). God wants you to be well-rounded, fully put together spiritually. The flip side of being complete is "lacking nothing."

God takes His Word (2 Tim. 3:16-17) and trials (1 Pet. 5:10) to bring about spiritual maturity in our lives.

Focusing on the Facts

1. Why must a Christian discipline himself to evaluate difficult circumstances as something joyful (see p. 42)?
2. Where was Paul when he said he had learned to be content in any situation (Phil. 4:11; see pp. 42-43)?
3. According to Hebrews 12:2, why did Jesus endure the cross (see p. 43)?
4. Why should we not expect to be free from trials (John 15:18, 20; see p. 44)?
5. Why can we, like the mother who gives birth, rejoice in the midst of trials (John 16:20-22; see p. 44)?
6. Explain why trials make Christians more sensitive to the Lord's presence (see p. 44).
7. What should motivate us to endure our trials with joy (Heb. 12:4; see p. 44)?
8. In spite of Paul's imprisonment in Rome and the criticism he received because of it, what things could he still rejoice in (Phil. 1:13, 18; see pp. 45-46)?

9. Why could Paul rejoice at the prospect of dying in the process of leading others to Christ (Phil. 2:17; see p. 46)?
10. Identify and define what trials are designed to produce (see p. 48).
11. Why does God allow increasingly greater trials in our lives (see p. 49)?
12. Will God put you through a trial you can't handle? Explain. Support your answer with Scripture (see p. 49).
13. Why was Christ willing to endure the cross (see p. 50)?
14. According to Hebrews 11:24-29, what did Moses choose over the comfort and treasures of Egypt? Why (see p. 50)?
15. What may be the consequence of refusing to submit to the trials God brings into your life (see p. 51)?
16. What should God's noble purpose of bringing us to spiritual maturity motivate us not to do? Why (see pp. 51-52)?
17. Differentiate between the means and the goal of a trial (see p. 52).
18. What is the result of submitting to the testing of our faith (see p. 53)?
19. Beside trials, what else does God use to perfect us (2 Tim. 3:16-17; see p. 53)?

Pondering the Principles

1. Memorize Romans 8:18: "The sufferings of this present time are not worthy to be compared with the glory which shall be revealed in us." If you are a Christian, you have an advantage in suffering that the unbeliever hasn't—the knowledge of a glorious future ahead of you. Paul was able to endure suffering because he had that eternal perspective. He said, "We faint not; but though our outward man perish, yet the inward man is renewed day by day. For our light affliction, which is but for a moment, worketh for us a far more exceeding and eternal weight of glory, while we look not at the things which are seen, but at the things which are not seen; for the things which are seen are temporal, but the things which are not seen are eternal" (2 Cor. 4:16-18).

2. Warren Wiersbe observed that if you value the temporal physical realm over the eternal spiritual realm, trials will make you bitter rather than better. Evaluate your response to trials and determine what realm you value the most. Be honest with your-

self because it is easy to deceive yourself into believing that you're following Christ when you are only admiring Him at a distance. Consider Amy Carmichael's poem on pages 47-48, which asks why we don't have the same wounds and scars Jesus had if we are truly following Him (cf. 2 Tim. 3:12).

3. The old hymn "Be Still, My Soul" has some meaningful words well worth pondering if you are encountering a trial or know someone who is:

> Be still, my soul—the Lord is on thy side!
> Bear patiently the cross of grief or pain;
> Leave to thy God to order and provide—
> In ev'ry change He faithful will remain.
> Be still, my soul—thy best, thy heavenly Friend
> Thru thorny ways leads to a joyful end.

Whatever that trial might be, leave it to the Lord to accomplish His purpose in your life. Praise Him for His wisdom, faithfulness, and love for you.

4
From Trouble to Triumph—Part 3

Outline

Introduction

Review
I. A Joyous Attitude (v. 2)
II. An Understanding Mind (v. 3)
III. A Submissive Will (v. 4)

Lesson
IV. A Believing Heart (vv. 5-8)
  A. The Prayer for Wisdom (v. 5*a*)
    1. The response to trials
    2. The resource in trials
      a) Proverbs 3:5-7
      b) Job 28:12-23
      c) James 5:16-18
  B. The Provider of Wisdom (v. 5*b*)
    1. Proverbs 2:2-6
    2. Jeremiah 29:11-14
    3. Matthew 7:7-11
    4. James 1:17
  C. The Promise of Wisdom (v. 5*c*)
    1. Psalm 81:10
    2. Mark 14:38
  D. The Prerequisite for Wisdom (vv. 6-8)
    1. The condition for the seeker (v. 6*a*)
    2. The contrast of the doubter (vv. 6*b*-8)
      a) The analogy (v. 6*b*)
        (1) Joshua 24:15
        (2) 1 Kings 18:21

Introduction

Many people who believe they are Christians and claim to know God find when facing the trials in their lives that they don't truly know Him. Their faith is revealed to be dead, nonsaving faith. Without the resources available to those who believe in God, they forsake their involvement in Christianity.

Trials are intended to prod people out of their security and awaken them to the fact that they either trust God or they don't. Trials affirm the legitimacy or the illegitimacy of our faith. That is what James has in mind in this opening section of his epistle. He is concerned throughout the entire epistle with the matter of living faith and offers a series of tests intended to reveal the legitimacy of someone's faith. The first test is the test of severe trials. We need to understand the strength or the genuineness of our own faith. Trials cannot destroy true faith; they only put it to the test and strengthen it.

Review

Trials have many purposes. God sends trials to humble us, to wean us from the world and focus on eternal things, to reveal the objects of our love, to teach us the value of God's blessing, to enable us to help others in their trials, to develop in us greater strength for greater usefulness, and to chasten us for our sin and push us toward perfection. James, however, is concerned with just one of the reasons God sends trials: to test the genuineness of our faith. The question that James really answers is, How can true faith endure any trial and remain intact? He presents five means to persevering in trials that are characteristic of true faith.

I. A JOYOUS ATTITUDE (v. 2; see pp. 42-48)

"My brethren, count it all joy, when ye fall into various trials."

II. AN UNDERSTANDING MIND (v. 3; see pp. 48-51)

"Knowing this, that the testing of your faith worketh patience."

III. A SUBMISSIVE WILL (v. 4; see pp. 51-53)

"Let patience have her perfect work, that ye may be perfect and entire, lacking nothing."

Lesson

If you are a Christian who is experiencing a trial and desire to keep a joyous attitude, an understanding mind, and a submissive will, but are still struggling, you probably lack the wisdom and the power to endure. You need wisdom—the practical insight needed to face the circumstances of life. You'll not be able to maintain the first three elements of a living faith unless God gives you more than just your human faculties to work with.

IV. A BELIEVING HEART (vv. 5-8)

A. The Prayer for Wisdom (v. 5a)

"If any of you lack wisdom, let him ask of God."

1. The response to trials

Divine wisdom is especially important when you are going through a trial and desire to endure it for the holy purposes of God. Human reasoning will provide few answers. To the Jewish reader at the time of this epistle, wisdom was the understanding needed to live life to the glory of God. It showed him how to live in obedience to the will and the Word of God.

When a believer is being tested, he will recognize his need for strength and will look for a greater resource to hold onto in the midst of the trial—God Himself. The search for wisdom is man's supreme search. For those of us who know and love the Lord, He provides that wisdom.

The kind of wisdom we are talking about is not philosophical speculation. We're talking about the absolutes of God's will, the divine wisdom that is pure and peaceable (James 3:17). Divine wisdom results in right conduct in all of life's matters. When some Christians go through troubles, their first response is to run to some other human resource. Although God may work through other believers, the Christian's initial response to trials should be to ask God directly for wisdom that will allow him to be joyous and submissive in finding and carrying out God's will.

Verse 5 is a command to pray that is not optional for the Christian. It is as mandatory as Paul's instruction to "pray without ceasing" (1 Thess. 5:17). Trials are intended to drive us to dependency on God by making us realize that we have no sufficient human resources.

2. The resource in trials

   a) Proverbs 3:5-7—"Trust in the Lord with all thine heart, and lean not unto thine own understanding. In all thy ways acknowledge him, and he shall direct thy paths. Be not wise in thine own eyes." When you're going through a trial, you must put your faith in God's wisdom and not in your own limited understanding.

   Trials have a way of enhancing your prayer life. They drive you to your knees to call on God for what you do not have and so desperately desire. God's intention is that you recognize the limitations of human reason.

b) Job 28:12-23—"Where shall wisdom be found? And where is the place of understanding? Man knoweth not its price; neither is it found in the land of the living. The depth saith, It is not in me; and the sea saith, It is not with me. It cannot be gotten for gold, neither shall silver be weighed for the price of it. It cannot be valued with the gold of Ophir, with the precious onyx, or the sapphire. The gold and the crystal cannot equal it; and the exchange of it shall not be for jewels of fine gold. No mention shall be made of coral, or of pearls, for the price of wisdom is above rubies. The topaz of Ethiopia shall not equal it, neither shall it be valued with pure gold. Whence, then, cometh wisdom? And where is the place of understanding? Seeing it is hidden from the eyes of all living, and kept close from the fowls of the air. Destruction and death say, We have heard its fame with our ears. God understandeth its way, and he knoweth the place of it."

The supernatural wisdom needed to understand the trials of life is not available in the world around us. If you need wisdom, you must acquire it from God. Job's friends meant well, but they didn't have the right answers. The right answers are available from God if we seek Him.

Seeking God for answers is more important than running to your friends or professional counselors for them. I believe the promise of wisdom for those who seek it is one of the greatest promises in all of Scripture. What more would we want than divine insight to understand and respond properly to every trial of life?

c) James 5:16-18—"The effectual, fervent prayer of a righteous man availeth much. Elijah was a man subject to like passions as we are, and he prayed earnestly that it might not rain; and it rained not in the earth by the space of three years and six months. And he prayed again, and the heaven gave rain, and the earth brought forth her fruit." God responds to the prayers of His children.

If you're going through some deep trouble in your life and it hasn't enriched your prayer life, then maybe the trouble will keep going on until you finally wake up and begin to do that. Wisdom is available if we ask God for it.

B. The Provider of Wisdom (v. 5b)

"God, who giveth to all men liberally and upbraideth not."

We have a gracious God who desires to give us that which we desire. The word *liberally* means "unconditionally and generously, without bargaining." I believe God will provide the wisdom to understand any trial if we will ask Him. If we don't ask, the Lord may allow the trial to continue until we demonstrate that we have learned to be dependent on Him through the trial. "Upbraideth not" means that God will not scold us for requesting wisdom. On the contrary, He will hold nothing back, giving generously without reservation.

1. Proverbs 2:2-6—"Incline thine ear unto wisdom, and apply thine heart to understanding; yea, if thou criest after knowledge, and liftest up thy voice for understanding; if thou seekest her as silver, and searchest for her as for hidden treasures; then shalt thou understand the fear of the Lord, and find the knowledge of God. For the Lord giveth wisdom; out of his mouth cometh knowledge and understanding." Although God makes wisdom available to those with a seeking heart, there's a sense in which He holds it back until you come and ask for it, demonstrating your dependence on Him.

2. Jeremiah 29:11-14—"I know the thoughts that I think toward you, saith the Lord, thoughts of peace, and not of evil, to give you an expected end. Then shall ye call upon me, and ye shall go and pray unto me, and I will hearken unto you. And ye shall seek me, and find me, when ye shall search for me with all your heart. And I will be found by you, saith the Lord."

3. Matthew 7:7-11—"Ask, and it shall be given you; seek, and ye shall find; knock, and it shall be opened unto you; for everyone that asketh receiveth; and he that seeketh findeth, and to him that knocketh it shall be

opened. Or what man is there of you whom, if his son ask bread, will he give him a stone? Or if he ask a fish, will he give him a serpent? If ye then, being evil, know how to give good gifts unto your children, how much more shall your Father, who is in heaven, give good things to them that ask him?" When you go through a difficult trial, go to God in prayer. He will generously give you the wisdom you need to understand that trial and properly respond to it.

4. James 1:17—"Every good gift, and every perfect gift is from above, and cometh down from the Father of lights, with whom there is no variableness, neither shadow of turning." It is God's nature to give generously without reservation. He does not give reluctantly because of our unworthiness. He gives graciously because of His goodness.

C. The Promise of Wisdom (v. 5c)

"It shall be given him."

If you lack wisdom, you're commanded to ask God for it. No wisdom needed for the believer's perseverance through a trial is ever withheld from that believer who asks. Isn't that a wonderful promise? Sometimes we don't ask; we do everything but ask God. We ought to be found on our knees crying out from our hearts for God to give us His direction.

1. Psalm 81:10—"I am the Lord thy God, who brought thee out of the land of Egypt; open thy mouth wide, and I will fill it." God wants to provide every needed resource for a believer in the midst of trial.

2. Mark 14:38—"Watch ye and pray, lest you enter into temptation [trials]." Jesus cautioned His disciples about entering trials and allowing them to become temptations. Prayer can enable us to endure a trial victoriously as we cast ourselves in dependency on God.

D. The Prerequisite for Wisdom (vv. 6-8)

1. The condition for the seeker (v. 6*a*)

"But let him ask in faith, nothing wavering."

The believer's request for wisdom should be offered in confident trust in God. The word *wavering* conveys the idea of doubting or, more literally, someone who is divided within himself as to his thinking. If he lacks wisdom, it's not God's fault. If you don't understand your trial—why your spouse died, your health is deteriorating, your finances are a mess, or you are having problems with your car, your job, or your children—you probably haven't asked God with unwavering faith to give you wisdom. Perhaps you have prayed somewhat insincerely with wrong motives like those whom James condemned as praying for things to consume on their lusts (4:3). Maybe you're not praying in accord with 1 Timothy 2:8, which says to pray "without wrath or doubting." You might be doubting whether God is able or willing to help. Unwavering faith simply believes that God is a sovereign, loving God who will supply everything needed for understanding the trial and being able to endure it. Whatever the trial is, you're to believe that God allowed it for His purpose and your spiritual maturity.

2. The contrast of the doubter (vv. 6*b*-8)

   a) The analogy (v. 6*b*)

   "He that wavereth is like a wave of the sea, driven with the wind and tossed."

   The wavering person who goes to God but doesn't believe that God can provide the wisdom is like the billowing, restless sea, moving back and forth with its endless tides, never able to settle.

   (1) Joshua 24:15—This mind-set is reminiscent of that which Joshua warned against when he addressed the Israelites, saying, "If it seem evil unto you to serve the Lord, choose you this day who ye will serve, whether the gods which your fathers served that were on the other side of the

river, or the gods of the Amorites, in whose land ye dwell; but as for me and my house, we will serve the Lord."

(2) 1 Kings 18:21—Elijah condemned the Israelites for their wavering faith, saying, "How long halt ye between two opinions? If the Lord be God, follow him; but if Baal, then follow him."

(3) 1 Corinthians 10:16-22—Paul condemned the Corinthians, some of whom were still involved in pagan worship and then participating in the Lord's Table.

(4) Revelation 3:16—People who claim to be Christians but who vacillate in their faith are like the lukewarm people who are neither hot nor cold, whom the Lord will spew out of His mouth. Such wavering people are like the surging sea.

b) The anticipation (v. 7)

"Let not that man think that he shall receive anything of the Lord."

There's no sense in such a person supposing he will receive anything from the Lord. The one who doubts God and isn't solidly committed to Him has the characteristics of an unbeliever or even a weak Christian who's acting like an unbeliever. When faced with a trial, an unbeliever who professes to know Christ will doubt God and get angry with Him and eventually sever his association with a church. A true Christian who is spiritually immature may respond in a similar manner because he reacts emotionally to his difficult circumstances and doesn't fully trust God. In the midst of trial he will not experience a joyous attitude, an understanding mind, a submissive will, or a believing heart. He will seem unable to ask for wisdom from God and unwilling to take advantage of the resources He has provided, never knowing the resolution available to him through faithful, persistent prayer to God.

65

c) The analysis (v. 8)

"A double-minded man is unstable in all his ways."

Being "double-minded" (Gk., *dipsuchos*) is the state of having one's soul or mind divided between God and the world. James 4:4, 8 says, "Friendship of the world is enmity with God. . . . Cleanse your hands, ye sinners; and purify your hearts, ye double mind-ed." A double-minded person is a hypocrite who believes in God periodically but who fails to place his trust in God when trials come and therefore receives nothing. Loving the world and trying to love God at the same time is impossible.

When you enter a trial, you will be able to endure it through divine wisdom and the confidence that God will give it freely and withhold nothing that is necessary for victory. The condition is that your faith be unwavering. Otherwise you will not only be unstable in every area of life, but you will not receive the wisdom you have requested. True stability in life comes to those who trust God in the midst of trials.

V. A HUMBLE SPIRIT (vv. 9-11)

A. The Exaltation of the Poor (v. 9)

"Let the brother of low degree rejoice in that he is exalted."

This is a command for the poor Christian to rejoice. The scattered Jewish believers to whom James wrote (v. 1) were victims of persecution and deprivation, so poverty among them would have been common. The Greek word translated "low degree" is used in the Septuagint, the Greek version of the Old Testament, to refer to the financially poor. "Rejoice" refers to the boasting of a privilege or a possession. It is the joy of legitimate pride. The poor Christian may have nothing in the material world to rejoice about, but he can rejoice in that he is exalted in the spiritual realm in his standing before God. He may be hungry, but he has the Bread of Life. He may be thirsty, but he has the Living Water. He may be poor, but he has eternal riches. He may be cast aside by men, but he has been received by God. He may have no home here, but he has a glorious home in the life to come. And in this life he may have trials, but God is using them to perfect and exalt him spiritually.

The Christian who is deprived can accept his trials because of the knowledge that God is exalting him spiritually through those difficult circumstances and because of the hope of receiving an incorruptible and undefiled inheritance that will never fade away (1 Pet. 1:4). Paul said that as children of God we are "heirs of God, and joint heirs with Christ—if so be that we suffer with him, that we may be also glorified together. For I reckon that the sufferings of this present time are not worthy to be compared with the glory which shall be revealed in us [when we are resurrected]" (Rom. 8:17-18). True riches are ours, so poverty is a short-lived trial that can be endured as we look ahead to a glorious time of exaltation. Don't find your joy in worldly circumstances and possessions or you will surely be disappointed if things change and you lose them. Rather, find your joy in the fact that God saved you and is moving you toward Christlikeness until you enter His presence.

B. The Humiliation of the Rich (vv. 10-11)

1. The acknowledgment of eternal values (v. 10a)

"But the rich, in that he is made low."

The well-to-do Christians, who don't seem to experience the trials of life related to poverty, can rejoice in their humiliation, because the trials they experience help them realize that their possessions can't buy true happiness and contentment and that their dependence is on the true riches of God's grace.

The poor Christian rejoices in the provision of God for his material needs and in the wealth of his spiritual position in Christ (Eph. 1:3), and the rich Christian rejoices in the humble knowledge that material blessings are only temporary and that spiritual riches are eternal. Both social classes of Christians can rejoice that God is no respecter of persons and that they have the privilege of being identified with Christ. Trials humble all believers to the same level of dependency on God. Money doesn't buy people out of their problems, although it may solve some economic ones. Whether to the poor or the rich, trials come into life to humble us to the point of recognizing that our resources are in God.

The great Lutheran commentator Lenski said, "Faith in Christ lifts the lowly brother beyond his trials to the great height of a position in the Kingdom of Christ, where as God's child he is rich and may rejoice and boast. Faith in Christ does an equally blessed thing for the rich brother: it fills him with the Spirit of Christ, the spirit of lowliness and true Christian humility. . . . As the poor brother forgets all his earthly poverty, so the rich brother forgets all his earthly riches. The two are equals by faith in Christ" (*The Interpretation of the Epistle to the Hebrews and the Epistle of James* [Minneapolis: Augsburg, 1966], pp. 534-35).

Equality is driven home through trials. When you lose a daughter, son, wife, or husband, it doesn't matter how much money you have. No amount is going to buy your way out of such a trial. Trials bring us to the same level of dependency on God and thus to the same level with each other so that we do not preoccupy ourselves with earthly things. We should not exalt those who have much over those who have little because earthly possessions are inadequate to buy us what we need spiritually.

2. The analogy of temporal values (vv. 10*b*-11)

"As the flower of the grass, he shall pass away. For the sun is no sooner risen with a burning heat, but it withereth the grass, and its flower falleth, and the grace of the fashion of it perisheth; so also shall the rich man fade away in his ways."

Wealthy people in general are usually not aware that their riches can't be taken with them. Only the rich who have been humbled before God realize that life is "a vapor that appeareth for a little time, and then vanisheth away" (James 4:14). The picture James paints is of the flowering grasses and flowers of Palestine (e.g., the anemone, the cyclamen, and the lily) that flourish with beautiful color in February and are dried up by May.

James borrows part of his illustration from Isaiah 40:6-8. He literally says the burning heat, which could refer to the scorching wind known as a sirocco, destroys the vegetation in its path. That is illustrative of the fury of death and the judgment of God that put an end to the rich man's earthly life and his material possessions. The rich man should rejoice in his trouble because it divorces him from dependency on his material resources. When they are burned up, he will have true riches, just as the poor man does. The wealthy Christian has a true spirit of humility that says, "I don't put my trust in the possessions of life, which pass so fast."

A Christian facing trials is to have a joyous attitude, an understanding mind, a submissive will, a believing heart, and a humble spirit that trusts not in his possessions but values the provision of God and His heavenly reward.

Focusing on the Facts

1. What do many unbelievers who claim to be Christians do when they encounter trials that reveal their lack of faith (see p. 58)?
2. What is the purpose for trials in relation to our sinning (see p. 58)?
3. Briefly describe wisdom (see pp. 59-60).
4. When a believer is being tested, what will he recognize and look for (see p. 60)?
5. Although God may work through other believers, where should Christians initially seek wisdom (see p. 60)?
6. Trials are intended to drive us to _____ on God by making us realize we have no _____ human resources (see p. 60).
7. If you are going through a trial that has not caused you to seek God in prayer, what may happen (see p. 62)?
8. Describe that aspect of God's character that should be an incentive for us to ask Him for wisdom (v. 5; see p. 62).
9. According to Jeremiah 29:11-14, how did God say He and His will would be found (see p. 62)?
10. How should the believer request wisdom from God (v. 6a; see p. 64)?

11. What analogy does James use for a doubting person? What can such a person expect to receive from God (see pp. 64-65)?
12. What is the "double-minded" person's loyalty divided between? What kind of friendship constitutes enmity with God (James 4:4; see p. 66)?
13. Identify "the brother of low degree" (James 1:9). Why can such a one rejoice (see pp. 66-67)?
14. Why can a rich Christian rejoice in having been spiritually humbled (see p. 67)?
15. Explain how trials reveal the equality of poor and rich Christians (see p. 68).

Pondering the Principles

1. When a trial comes into your life, do you automatically seek God's wisdom, desiring to know what He wants you to learn by it and how to properly handle it? If not, maybe you haven't established a close relationship with the Lord during the good times. When He becomes your best Friend, it will only be natural for you to seek Him for comfort and guidance when troubles arise. James 5:13 commands us to pray when we are suffering. And if we have fallen to the point where we are so spiritually weak that we can't pray effectively, verse 14 instructs us to call the spiritually strong to pray for us. According to the promise of the Lord in verse 15, He will restore our strength. Verse 16 encourages us to share our burdens and any sins that would destroy Christian unity and to support one another in prayer. Are you daily utilizing the power of prayer to maintain your spiritual strength so that when a trial comes along you will be better prepared to handle it?

2. Meditate on Ephesians 1-2 and 1 Timothy 6:6-12. If you are a Christian with limited financial means you can rejoice in the wealth of your spiritual position in Christ. Rather than making it your life ambition to acquire wealth, seek to have an attitude of contentment as you pursue godliness. If you are financially secure, you can rejoice in that God has graciously chosen you to be a child of His kingdom. Rather than being preoccupied with trying to conserve your wealth for you and your family, invest it into the kingdom. Make sure that you are actively involved in ministry yourself and are not merely giving your money to the Lord to avoid giving your time.

5
Whose Fault Is Our Temptation?

Outline

Introduction
A. The Qualification Regarding Temptations
B. The Question About Temptations
   1. Asked
   2. Answered

Lesson
  I. The Nature of Evil (v. 13)
   A. The Stated Contrast
   B. The Supposed Contradictions
     1. The tally by David
     2. The testing of Jesus
     3. The teaching on prayer
  II. The Nature of Man (v. 14)
   A. The Analogy of Being Trapped
   B. The Agency Bringing About Temptation
     1. Its individuality
     2. Its identity
  III. The Nature of Lust (vv. 15-16)
   A. The Explanation (v. 15)
     1. The process of lust
       a) Desire
       b) Deception
       c) Design
       d) Disobedience
     2. The prevention of lust
     3. The product of lust
   B. The Exhortation (v. 16)

IV. The Nature of God (v. 17)
   A. His Goodness and Graciousness (v. 17a)
   B. His Stability and Steadfastness (v. 17b)

Conclusion

Introduction

James 1:14 begins with these words: "Every man is tempted." All of us can give testimony to the truthfulness of that statement. Everyone is tempted. Temptation is the common experience of every human being, whether he is a Christian or not. Paul says in 1 Corinthians 10:13 that temptations are "common to man." One ancient writer said that even when we are saved, we must remember that our baptism did not drown our flesh. How we deal with the battle of temptation is another mark of the genuineness of our faith or the lack of it.

A. The Qualification Regarding Temptations

James makes a sudden change from verse 12 to 13. James had been referring to trials with the Greek noun *peirasmos*, but then he used the same word to refer to temptations. The trials that the Lord allows into our lives to strengthen us can also become temptations, which, rather than being a means to spiritual growth, can become a solicitation to evil. Every difficult thing that comes into my life either strengthens me because I obey God and stay confident in His care and power, or it leads me to doubt God and disobey His Word. The difference between a trial and a temptation is how you respond to it. Every trial has the potential to become a temptation.

B. The Question About Temptations

1. Asked

We are thus faced with a decision: Will we obediently persevere in trials, or will we listen to the voice suggesting that the easy way out is disobedience? If we fall into sin, whose fault is it? Is it God's fault for allowing the trials? Is it His fault for having created us the way we are? Is it the fault of our circumstances? The issue of who is to blame for temptation is the heart of this passage. It is an age-old question.

2. Answered

Although it is an ancient belief that God is responsible for our temptation and sin, James forbade such a thought. In fact, he implied that someone who intimately knows God grieves over his sin, readily confesses it, and wouldn't think of blaming God for it.

James warned against rationalizing our sin and blaming God in the midst of our battle against temptation. "Let no one say" is in the middle voice in the Greek text and could be translated "let no one say to himself" or "let no one excuse himself." When you are fighting temptation and near to yielding, don't make the excuse that you are being tempted by God.

The Greek preposition in the phrase translated "tempted of God" is not *hupo*, the preposition of direct agency, referring to whomever is the direct cause of something; it is *apo*, a preposition of origin conveying the idea of remoteness. Assuming that no one would accuse God of directly causing him to sin, James is saying that we should not even think of God as the remote origin of our temptation, the ultimate cause of our sins. Most men don't go as far as to see God as the direct tempter, but they do believe God is indirectly to blame by having permitted the situation and the possibility of failure. But God is not the near agency of temptation, nor is He even its remote cause. Don't ever look at yourself as a victim of God's providence.

Lesson

To support that exhortation in verse 13, James gives us four proofs in verse 13-17 showing why God is not responsible for temptation or sin.

I. THE NATURE OF EVIL (v. 13)

"Let no man say when he is tempted, I am tempted of God; for God cannot be tempted with evil, neither tempteth he any man."

A. The Stated Contrast

The Greek translated "cannot be tempted" implies that God is inexperienced with evil because He has no capacity for it or vulnerability to it. The mention of "evil" without an article refers to the whole realm of evil, none of which is able to penetrate the holy nature of God. All evil repulses God because its stands in opposition to His holiness. Although Scripture is replete with statements of God's holiness (Lev. 19:2; 20:26; Isa. 6:3; 1 Pet. 1:16), perhaps Habakkuk 1:13 is the clearest statement that evil cannot permeate God's holiness: "Thou art of purer eyes than to behold evil, and canst not look on iniquity." The nature of evil makes it impossible for God to be tempted, or to tempt someone else, which would indicate that He has a delight in seeing someone else do evil. He who knows no evil cannot delight in evil.

B. The Supposed Contradictions

1. The tally by David

Second Samuel 24:1 seems to contradict James 1:13: "The anger of the Lord was kindled against Israel, and he incited David against them, to say, Go, number Israel and Judah." David committed a sin by numbering his people and trusting in their military might rather than God's. However, 1 Chronicles 21:1 clarifies that "Satan stood up against Israel, and enticed David to number Israel." Satan is accurately identified as the tempter of David. The broader picture Samuel gives is that God allowed it to happen because David had the choice to respond or not respond to the enticement of Satan. And James clarifies that not only is God not directly involved in inciting us to sin, but He is not even remotely responsible.

2. The testing of Jesus

Matthew 4:1 says the Holy Spirit led Jesus "into the wilderness to be tested by the devil." One might believe God was leading Him into temptation, but He wasn't, because none of the tests were temptations designed to lead Jesus into sin. Rather they proved Him to be the Son of God.

3. The teaching on prayer

The request of Matthew 6:13 to "lead us not into temptation" has to do with trials. It's an emotional plea of the saint who's praying, "God, don't lead me into any trial that is more than I can bear." The Lord's answer is found in 1 Corinthians 10:13, which says, "There hath no temptation [trial] taken you but such as is common to man; but God is faithful, who will not permit you to be tempted above that ye are able, but will, with the temptation, also make the way to escape, that ye may be able to bear it." When we pray, "Lead us not into trials or temptation," we are simply asking God to do what He has already promised to do in never giving us more than we can bear.

God allows temptation to go on, and men like David have to make a choice. But God Himself does not tempt. He allows us to be tested, even as He allowed Christ to be tested. But He doesn't allow more than we are able to bear, and He provides an avenue of victory that we are free to choose.

II. THE NATURE OF MAN (v. 14)

"But every man is tempted, when he is drawn away of his own lust, and enticed."

Temptation doesn't come from God but from within. The use of the present tense in the Greek test implies that every person goes through repeated experiences of temptation.

A. The Analogy of Being Trapped

"Drawn away" is used in hunting contexts of animals being lured into traps. "Enticed" is a term used of catching fish and means "to capture" or "to catch with bait." In 2 Peter 2:14 and 18, the latter term is translated "to beguile" and "to allure." Every person is tempted when the trap of sin is baited with that which appeals to our lust. A person's lust responding to an enticing bait deceptively draws him away to the point where he is trapped.

Animals are often caught by an inviting-looking bait in a trap or on a hook that is disguised. Instead of the anticipated pleasure of enjoying the bait, the animal experiences the pain of capture and death. Likewise, temptation promises a tasty indulgence as it lures the victim into its deadly trap.

B. The Agency Bringing About Temptation

What pulls us so strongly to the bait? It's not God. And it's not Satan, his demons, or the world's evil system that entice us to sin, although they bait the hook. It is the lustful nature of man that pulls us to take hold of it. Our flesh, our fallen nature, has a desire for evil.

1. Its individuality

"His own" implies that the nature of lust may be different for each person. One person's passion is another person's repulsion. I see people who are driven into homosexuality by their lust, but that sin doesn't entice me. Some temptations are more alluring to us than others.

2. Its identity

"Lust" (Gk., *epithumia*) refers to the strong desire of the soul to enjoy or acquire something. The use of the preposition *hupo* before the noun indicates that the direct agent of temptation is lust. Lust is the cause of our sinning—not God, and not even the devil, demons, or wicked people. The latter three surrounded Christ through His entire life, yet He never sinned because He had no lust. Nothing put on the hook attracted Him in any way. The problem is not the tempter without—it's the traitor within. Each person's soul has its own patterns of fleshly desire as a result of his environment, upbringing, and personal choices. Man's human nature has the propensity to desire what will satisfy it. And if lured to things outside the will of God, his lust will tempt him to bite the bait and be caught by the hook of sin.

Pogo, the cartoon character, was famous for saying, "We have met the enemy and he is us." From a spiritual perspective the problem is that even though we've been redeemed and have received a new nature, we still have an enemy within. The resident passion of the flesh, not God, is responsible for our being tempted to sin.

III. THE NATURE OF LUST (vv. 15-16)

A. The Explanation (v. 15)

"Then when lust hath conceived, it bringeth forth sin; and sin, when it is finished, bringeth forth death."

The third reason God is not the source of sin is found in the nature of lust. James shifts metaphors from hunting and fishing to childbirth. He personifies lust resulting in sin as a mother conceiving a child. Most people think of sin as an individual act or behavior. God is saying that sin is not an act; it is the result of a process.

1. The process of lust

a) Desire

Sin starts with lust (Gk., *epithumia*, "strong desire"). Desire is related to emotion. It is a desire to be satisfied by acquiring something. It may be something you saw in a jewelry store, a car dealership, a shopping mall, or a real-estate office. You have an emotional longing to possess what you saw.

b) Deception

Temptation next affects your mind through deception. You begin to justify and rationalize your right to possess what you desire. Your mind is deceived into believing that fulfilling your lust will satisfy you and meet your need.

c) Design

Next your will gets involved in plotting how you're going to get what you want. The Greek word translated "conceived" (*sullambanō*) means "to grasp together" and refers in a technical sense to a woman's taking hold of a man's seed and thereby conceiving a child. When lust, so to speak, is seduced by the prostitution of that baited hook, it becomes pregnant in the womb of a person's will.

d) Disobedience

Finally the act of sin occurs. The birth of a child follows a similar process. First there is a desire between husband and wife to have a child. That is followed by the decision to do so and the act of the will in bringing about conception, all of which result in the birth of the child. Temptation follows that sequence until it results in sinful behavior.

The Greek word translated "bringeth forth" (*tiktō*) means "to give birth." Lust gives birth to sin because it influenced the mind to justify sin, and the mind convinced the will to give birth to sinful behavior.

Dealing a Deathblow to Sinful Desires

At what point do we deal with sin? Not at the point of behavior—for that's too late—but at the point of desire. It's the person who is able to control his emotional responses who is able to deal effectively with sin. Or if the person who is being bombarded by negative emotional responses has a mind that is sanctified, those desires can be deactivated before they can be activated by the will. But once they capture the will, their birth is inevitable. You must deal with lustful emotions if you want to effectively deal with sin in your life. If you expose your emotions to the baited hook, you may find yourself getting hooked unless you take immediate action.

2. The prevention of lust

So many things in our evil society attempt to work on our emotions: movies, television, books, music, clothing, advertisements—all the alluring sights and sounds that attract our attention are designed to capture the emotions. For example, advertising executives know that buying is ultimately an emotional decision. Few people know or even care about the mechanics of a car being advertised, yet they are impressed by a car that looks like a race car, or by a pretty woman behind the wheel, or by other kinds of emotional bait that has nothing to do with how the car functions.

We need to guard our minds, emotions, and wills, "bringing into captivity every thought to the obedience of Christ" (2 Cor. 10:5). We need to seek God's will by meditating on His Word and letting His will become ours. An unprotected, uncontrolled, and unyielded mind is going to be filled with evil desires that will result in evil deeds. So we must control how our emotions and minds respond to the tempting bait they encounter. That's where sin begins.

In spite of that, emotional responses can be a wonderful blessing if they are expressed in a godly manner. Music elicits primarily an emotional response, and Christians have the privilege of receiving and experiencing the emotional enjoyment that comes from hearing and producing music that honors God. But we cannot continually expose our emotions to that which lures us away from the things of God without paying the price. And because we can't always regulate what our emotions are exposed to, it is necessary for us to have "the mind of Christ" (1 Cor. 2:16), set "on things above, not on things on the earth" (Col. 3:2), saturated with the "word of Christ" (Col. 3:16), and renewed and able to transform us rather than conform us to the world (Rom. 12:2). We need to love the Lord with all our minds (Mark 12:30). If our minds feed on the Word of God and our emotions are under the Spirit's control, we're going to stop sin before it ever starts. If we fail in those areas, we will conceive sin and carry out unrighteous acts.

3. The product of lust

James says that "sin, when it is finished, bringeth forth death." The Greek word translated "bringeth forth" (*apakueō*) means "to give birth to." Lust conceives and gives birth to sin, which ultimately brings forth death. Romans 6:23 says, "The wages of sin is death." The kind of death sin results in is spiritual death—the eternal separation of the soul from God. (Physical death is the separation of the soul from the body.)

James is not specifically talking about Christians or non-Christians but is making the general statement that sin produces death. Although sin in a believer will not result in spiritual death, it can result in physical death (1 Cor. 11:30; 1 John 5:16). The hope that you're bringing some satisfying behavior to life by sinning is a false hope.

B. The Exhortation (v. 16)

"Do not err, my beloved brethren."

James is saying that we're to stop being led astray and deceived. The Greek word translated "err" gives us our English word *planet.* It refers to something that wanders. James warns us not to wander from the truth by thinking that sin is God's fault and doesn't have consequences. We must not blame God for our sin, but ourselves. We need to realize that we have an enemy within us—the lust of our fallen human nature. We cannot expose our emotions to everything that lures us and let our minds become captive to those things. We've got to know where the problem is and deal with it at that level. Fill your mind with the things of God so that temptations can never mate with your feelings and conceive sin in your will.

IV. THE NATURE OF GOD (v. 17)

A. His Goodness and Graciousness (v. 17a)

"Every good gift and every perfect gift is from above."

The only things that come from God are good and perfect. God could never produce evil, because His nature is good. Rather, He produces unending good. Whereas we possess a nature that gives rise to sin, God does not. Why would we try to satisfy ourselves with baited hooks that result in death when God is pouring out everything we could ever want for our satisfaction? Only a fool would be lured away by a baited trap when all the goodness of God is available by His grace. Likewise, our flesh can be compared to a well of stagnant water. It is ludicrous to believe that we could be satisfied by drinking from it when we can come to the fountain of Living Water Himself who gives us every good and perfect gift.

The double use of "every" and "gift" emphasize the all-inclusiveness of God's graciousness. Two different Greek words are used for "gift." *Dosis* refers to the act of giving, and *dōrēma* refers to the object that is given. Every act of giving on God's part and every gift He gives is sufficient, lacking nothing, beneficial, and complete.

Satan deceived Eve by implying that God was holding out on her and that she better grab what satisfaction she could by eating from the forbidden tree and supposedly becoming like God (Gen. 3:1-6). She believed that lie, and the child of sin was conceived and born, bringing forth both spiritual death and physical death for the human race.

B. His Stability and Steadfastness (v. 17*b*)

"And cometh down from the Father of lights, with whom is no variableness, neither shadow of turning."

James called God "the Father of lights." That was an ancient Jewish reference to God as the Creator. The lights referred to are the sun, moon, and stars. James chose that title because it fit his illustration. God created the celestial bodies, but with Him there's no variation or shifting. From our perspective the sun, moon, and stars move, disappear, change in shape, or vary in intensity—their benefit to us coming and going. But God isn't like that. His brilliant light of glory and gracious goodness does not change. God doesn't pass from one condition to another or change like shadows do as the sun moves. His grace never goes dark. First John 1:5 says, "God is light, and in him is no darkness at all." Malachi 3:6 says, "I am the Lord, I change not." There are no days when He stops giving to men. The flow of good things from God never varies or stops.

Conclusion

A fish that has eaten takes no bait. So if you're feeding on the divine resources available to every believer, you'll find that the baited hook of temptation holds little attraction for you. Fill up on divine gifts. Eighteenth-century hymn writer Robert Robinson wrote,

> Come, Thou Fount of ev'ry blessing,
> Tune my heart to sing Thy grace;
> Streams of mercy, never ceasing,
> Call for songs of loudest praise.

The streams of God's mercy never cease. Nothing can eclipse His goodness or stop His benevolence. Knowing that, don't take the devil's bait and give birth to deadly sin. Rather, receive the good that God wants to give you.

Focusing on the Facts

1. Who faces temptation (James 1:14; see p. 72)?
2. What is the difference between a trial and a temptation (see p. 72)?
3. What does James warn us against doing when we experience trials (James 1:13; see p. 73)?
4. What should we never look at ourselves as victims of? Why (see p. 73)?
5. Why can't God be tempted with evil? Support your answer with Scripture (see p. 73).
6. Cite some biblical examples that supposedly contradict the fact that God does not tempt us. How can they be resolved (see pp. 74-75)?

7. What promise shows that God knows the limit of the trials we can handle (see p. 75)?
8. According to James 1:14, where does temptation come from (see p. 75)?
9. What analogies does James allude to in verse 14 to make his point (see pp. 75-76)?
10. Although man's fallen nature has a desire for evil, is every person's lust the same? Explain (see p. 76).
11. How does James personify lust in verse 15 (see p. 77)?
12. Explain the four-step process of lust leading to sin (see pp. 77-78).
13. At what point should we deal with sin? Why (see p. 78)?
14. How can we guard our minds, emotions, and wills? Support your answer with Scripture (see p. 79).
15. When are emotional responses a wonderful blessing (see p. 79)?
16. What does sin result in? Could that include the believer? Explain (see p. 80).
17. What is it about God's nature that teaches us He would never tempt us to commit evil (v. 17; see pp. 80-82)?

Pondering the Principles

1. We tend to justify our sins and blame others for making us commit them. A brief look at Adam and Eve's responses to God about their disobedience reveals that human trait (Gen. 3:12-13). Our society has so intensified that tendency that we tend to take little if any responsibility for our actions. Are you influenced by that kind of thinking? Do you find yourself blaming demons or ungodly people for your sin? Or are you sensitive to sin and willing to take full responsibility for it as you confess it to the Lord? Meditate on the prayer of confession Daniel offered in Daniel 9. Ask God to enable you to follow Daniel's example of "a broken and a contrite heart" (Ps. 51:17).

2. Sin must be dealt with as soon as your emotions and mind begin lusting for something that is outside the will of God. Satan offered Jesus the glory of ruling "all the kingdoms of the world" (Matt. 4:8-9), but the Lord was not willing to become subservient to Satan. He knew the promise of Psalm 2:7-8: "Thou art my Son; this day have I begotten thee. Ask of me, and I shall give

thee the nations for thine inheritance, and the uttermost parts of the earth for thy possession." Are you lusting for a position, possession, or perversion that is not in accord to God's timing or will? To stop that illicit desire before it gives birth to sin and chastisement, search God's Word to know His will (Ps. 119:11; Matt. 4:10). Immediately change your course of direction and avoid any situation that might tempt your emotions and allow your mind to justify your sin (Gen. 39:7-12; 2 Timothy 2:22). Thank the Lord that He can give you victory over temptation and sin as you saturate your mind with His Word and yield yourself to the control of His Spirit.

6
Born to Holiness

Outline

Introduction
A. Man's Need for Holiness
    1. James 1:13-17
    2. Romans 3:9-18
       a) Man's sinfulness stated
       b) Man's sinfulness illustrated
    3. Ephesians 2:1-3
B. God's Provision of Holiness
    1. Expressed
       a) The internal corruption
          (1) Jeremiah 17:9
          (2) Jeremiah 13:23
          (3) 1 Corinthians 2:14
       b) The internal correction
          (1) Jeremiah 31:31-33
          (2) Ephesians 2:5-6
          (3) Romans 6:4
          (4) Ephesians 4:24
    2. Examined
       a) The search for new life
          (1) The silent question
          (2) The symbolic question
       b) The source of new life
          (1) Identified
          (2) Illustrated

Lesson
I. The Nature of Regeneration
   A. The Energizing of Regeneration
   B. The Event of Regeneration
   C. The Effect of Regeneration
II. The Source of Regeneration
   A. The Will of God
   B. The Response of Faith
      1. To God's sovereign will
         a) John 1:12-13
         b) John 6:44
      2. To God's gracious love
         a) 1 John 4:19
         b) 1 John 3:1
III. The Means of Regeneration
   A. Stated
   B. Supported
      1. 1 Thessalonians 2:13
      2. Titus 3:5
   C. Specified
      1. 2 Corinthians 6:7
      2. Colossians 1:5
      3. 2 Timothy 2:15
IV. The Purpose of Regeneration
   A. Identified
   B. Illustrated

Introduction

A. Man's Need for Holiness

Hebrews 12:14 says that without holiness no one will see the Lord. To have a relationship with God one must become holy. Jesus emphasized that the goal of every believer is holiness, saying, "Be ye, therefore, perfect, even as your Father, who is in heaven, is perfect" (Matt. 5:48). Peter quoted God's command in Leviticus 11:44 when he said, "Be ye holy; for I am holy" (1 Pet. 1:16).

People are not holy—that's obvious. They are sinful. They do not think right, speak right, or act right according to God's perfect standards. They do not rightly perceive God,

His truth, His will, or themselves. Most people are oblivious to the fact that they are unrighteous. They do not willingly agree with the diagnosis of Scripture that they are sinful and are in need of holiness. Indirectly, men push off onto God the responsibility for their sinfulness. But verses 13-17 of James 1 have shown us that we have no one to blame but ourselves for our own sinfulness.

1. James 1:13-17—James has shown that man is filled with lust, which produces sin and results in death. To know God and enter into His eternal presence, we must be holy. Yet man is unholy and his sinful nature produces lust and evil.

2. Romans 3:9-18—Paul quotes several psalms revealing man's need for salvation because he is under the control of sin.

   a) Man's sinfulness stated

   "Both Jews and Greeks . . . are all under sin; as it is written, There is none righteous, no, not one" (vv. 9-10). There is not one human being created in this world since the Fall of Adam who is right with God. Verses 11-12 say, "There is none that understandeth, there is none that seeketh after God. They are all gone out of the way, they are together become unprofitable; there is none that doeth good, no, not one." No one fully comprehends that which God requires and is able to carry it out. The bent of man is to seek sin rather than God. John 3:19 says, "Men loved darkness rather than light, because their deeds were evil." When men divert themselves from the path that God ordained for righteousness, they become "unprofitable," or useless.

   b) Man's sinfulness illustrated

   "Their throat is an open sepulcher; with their tongues they have used deceit; the poison of asps is under their lips; whose mouth is full of cursing and bitterness" (vv. 13-14). The sin of such people stinks like a dead corpse. The throat, mouth, tongue, and lips identify the means of expression for their sinfulness. "Their feet are swift to shed blood; destruction and misery are in their ways; and the way of peace have they not known. There is no fear [reverence] of God before their eyes" (vv. 15-18). Man is unwilling to follow God's law and unable to keep it.

Therefore all mankind is without excuse and stands "guilty before God" (v. 19). There is no way that man, through his own efforts of keeping the law of God, can be justified by God. The law simply produces an awareness of sin; it doesn't produce righteousness (v. 20).

3. Ephesians 2:1-3—Paul told the Ephesians that before they believed they were "dead in trespasses and sins; in which in times past ye walked according to the course of this world, according to the prince of the power of the air, the spirit that now worketh in the sons of disobedience" (vv. 1-2). Because of sin man is characterized as being dead. His daily conduct is dictated by the world's evil system, which is ruled by Satan. As unbelievers, we functioned "in the lusts of our flesh, fulfilling the desires of the flesh and of the mind, and were by nature the children of wrath" (v. 3). Unbelievers are the object of God's judgment.

To have a right relationship to God, man needs to be holy. And if by chance he recognizes that he is not holy, he wrongly tends to blame God for his circumstances. So man apart from God is in a desperate state.

B. God's Provision of Holiness

James 1:18 says, "Of his [God's] own will begot he us with the word of truth, that we should be a kind of first fruits of his creatures." That simple verse speaks of the richness of the new birth. James introduces the subject of regeneration in verse 18 to show that God doesn't lead people into sin but into a life of holiness.

The question is asked: What can man do to change his situation? Scripture makes clear that external changes are not enough. Man cannot by some resolution determine that he's going to obey the law of God and work his way out of his spiritual deadness. Because he cannot give himself new life, he needs to be recreated. He needs a new heart, a new nature. In the words of Jesus, he needs to be "born again" (John 3:3). He needs to start over as if, in the words of Nicodemus, he could crawl back into his mother's womb and come out with a different nature (John 3:4). Since holiness is the condition for fellowship with God, sinful man in his fallen condition cannot experience that fellowship. And because God won't accept his corrupt nature, he needs a new and holy life.

1. Expressed

    a) The internal corruption

        Being born again is not simply adding something to an existing life. That would be like putting a ribbon on a sow. The change that man needs is not external, like a new suit of clothes; it's a total transformation. To enter into a right relationship with God demands that a person be recreated by God Himself. Both the Old and New Testaments affirm that.

        (1) Jeremiah 17:9—"The heart is deceitful above all things, and desperately wicked."

        (2) Jeremiah 13:23—"Can the Ethiopian change his skin, or the leopard his spots? Then may ye also do good, that are accustomed to do evil." Man cannot change his bent toward evil any more than a person or animal can change the appearance of their skin. Doing what is right demands a total transformation.

        (3) 1 Corinthians 2:14—Man has to have a change at the very core of his being. The natural or unregenerate man "receiveth not the things of the Spirit of God." An unbeliever cannot understand or accept them because he's spiritually dead. He needs a new life.

b) The internal correction

    (1) Jeremiah 31:31-33—"Behold, the days come, saith the Lord, that I will make a new covenant with the house of Israel, and with the house of Judah, not according to the covenant I made with their fathers in the day that I took them by the hand to bring them out of the land of Egypt . . . but this shall be the covenant that I will make with the house of Israel: After those days, saith the Lord, I will put my law in their inward parts, and write it in their hearts, and will be their God, and they shall be my people." God has to change a person's heart because no one can do that on his own.

    (2) Ephesians 2:5-6—"Even when we were dead in sins, [God] hath made us alive together with Christ . . . and hath raised us up together." That's a spiritual resurrection to new life.

    (3) Romans 6:4—When you put your faith in Christ, you die to your old self but rise to "walk in newness of life." The old life has to be totally done away with, and a new life has to come.

    (4) Ephesians 4:24—"Put on the new man, which after God is created in righteousness and true holiness." When you come to salvation, you become a new person on the inside.

2. Examined

    a) The search for new life

        (1) The silent question

        John 3 records the encounter between Jesus and Nicodemus, whom Jesus recognized as one of the prominent religious teachers of Israel (v. 10): "There was a man of the Pharisees, named Nicodemus, a ruler of the Jews; the same came to Jesus by night, and said unto him, Rabbi, we know that thou art a teacher come from God; for no man can do these miracles that thou doest, except God be with him" (vv. 1-2). Although he was a man of great esteem, Nicodemus recognized Jesus as one who was significantly above him.

Before Nicodemus could ask his question, Jesus answered it, for He knows what is in every man's heart: "Verily, verily, I say unto thee, Except a man be born again, he cannot see the kingdom of God" (v. 3). Although he was a spiritual leader in Israel, Nicodemus knew he had not entered into the kingdom of God because he had no internal spiritual confirmation of that. Jesus told him in effect that even though he was a trusted and respected teacher he would have to start all over by being spiritually reborn.

(2) The symbolic question

"Nicodemus saith unto him, How can a man be born when he is old? Can he enter the second time into his mother's womb, and be born?" (v. 4). Nicodemus was not referring to the physical realm. He was simply using veiled parabolic language, a common rabbinical teaching device, by continuing the metaphor of birth that Jesus had introduced. He was asking how anyone—let alone a religious expert—who had spent so many years in a religion could ever undo all his religious beliefs and start again. If you have had the opportunity to witness to someone who has been entrenched in a religion for a long period, you understand the mind-set of Nicodemus.

b) The source of new life

(1) Identified

"Jesus answered, Verily, verily, I say unto thee, Except a man be born of water and of the Spirit, he cannot enter into the kingdom of God" (v. 5). Entering the kingdom (salvation) is accomplished by an agent outside yourself—water and the Spirit. "Water" refers to the water of salvation men-

91

tioned in Ezekiel 36:25-27 (cf. Jer. 24:7), where God promised Israel, "Then will I sprinkle clean water upon you, and ye shall be clean; from all your filthiness, and from all your idols, will I cleanse you. A new heart also will I give you, and a new spirit will I put within you; and I will take away the stony heart out of your flesh, and I will give you an heart of flesh. And I will put my Spirit within you, and cause you to walk in my statutes, and ye shall keep mine ordinances, and do them." Jesus was speaking in familiar terms to Nicodemus, for he knew the Old Testament promises of salvation and restoration mentioned in passages such as Ezekiel 36. He told Nicodemus that he must have an internal cleansing by God's Holy Spirit. Similarly Paul spoke of "the washing of water by the word" (Eph. 5:26) and "the washing of regeneration, and renewing of the Holy Spirit" (Titus 3:5) in reference to salvation. Salvation is a sovereign cleansing that comes from God who sends the Holy Spirit to indwell your heart and give you new life.

(2) Illustrated

Jesus went on to say, "That which is born of the flesh is flesh; and that which is born of the Spirit is spirit. Marvel not that I said unto thee, Ye must be born again. The wind bloweth where it willeth, and thou hearest the sound of it, but canst not tell from where it cometh, and where it goeth; so is every one that is born of the Spirit" (vv. 6-8). Jesus was saying, "Only the Spirit of God can produce spiritual life—that shouldn't be too surprising. And the spiritual regeneration He sovereignly accomplishes is like the wind—it's not something you can see or control."

Sinful man needs a new heart or, in New Testament terms, a new nature: "If any man be in Christ, he is a new creation; old things are passed away; behold, all things are become new" (2 Cor. 5:17). A new birth is essential. That's what salvation is: God sovereignly and graciously cleansing the sinner to restore his relationship with Him and planting His Spirit in him, thus enabling him to obey the will of God. That's the purpose of regeneration.

Lesson

I. THE NATURE OF REGENERATION

A. The Energizing of Regeneration

Man's predicament seems like a vicious cycle: he doesn't know God because his sin separates him from God. Man generally doesn't recognize his unholiness, and if he does, he blames God for it. So one might wonder how he's ever going to break out of that cycle. It's not by attempting to meet higher standards or better ethics in his own power. The phrase "of his own will begot he us" in James 1:18 tells us that man needs divine intervention to wash away his sin and energize his new life. That's the nature of regeneration. It's God's giving new life to us as spiritually reborn beings. Using the same Greek word for birth that he uses in verse 15, James here in verse 18 repeats the metaphor of giving birth. Note the contrast: rather than bringing forth death as sin does, God brings forth new spiritual life.

B. The Event of Regeneration

"Begot he us" looks back to when we were given new life as children of God. Theologian Louis Berkhof defines that new birth in these words: "Regeneration is that act of God by which the principle of the new life is implanted in man, and the governing disposition of the soul is made holy" (*Systematic Theology* [Grand Rapids: Eerdmans, 1941], p. 469). Regeneration is a total transformation. In fact, the apostle Peter says we "become partakers of the divine nature" (2 Pet. 1:4). God shares His life with us and imputes His righteousness to our account. Although we have yet to receive the fullness of our salvation (glorification and freedom from the presence of sin), a new-life principle is implanted in us in a moment of time. Salvation in that sense is an event, not a process.

C. The Effect of Regeneration

Because salvation is a spiritual event it is imperceptible to others. That's why it can be difficult to tell believers from unbelievers or, in the words of Jesus, to separate the wheat from the tares (Matt. 13:27-30). Salvation is, however, known through its effect. Although we can't see someone become regenerated, we can see the result. His new life enables and motivates him to overcome sin and live righteously. No longer does sin have dominion over him (Rom. 6:14). Rather he willingly follows a new master—Jesus Christ—who came for the express purpose of giving life to the spiritually dead (John 10:10).

II. THE SOURCE OF REGENERATION

A. The Will of God

God the Father, mentioned in James 1:17 as the source of every good and perfect gift, is the One who begot us (v. 18). "Of his own will" occurs first in word order in the Greek text, making it emphatic. That highlights the sovereign will of God as the source of this new life. It couldn't be any other way, because a dead person can't give life to himself. Regeneration results from the grace of the Giver, not the desire of the receiver, and even the desire of the receiver is prompted by God's grace (Eph. 2:8). Therefore salvation is wholly the choice and work of almighty God. So when a person is saved, God deserves all the credit.

B. The Response of Faith

1. To God's sovereign will

From a human perspective it appears as if we are active in believing and receiving Christ.

a) John 1:12-13—"As many as received him, to them gave he power [authority] to become the children of God, even to them that believe on his name; who were born, not of blood, nor of the will of the flesh, nor of the will of man, but of God." You believed and received because it was the will of God. Similarly, no child has ever been born into the world because he or she wanted to be born. The birth of a child is strictly the decision of its parents.

    b) John 6:44—Jesus indicated that spiritual birth is ultimately the decision of the Father: "No man can come to me, except the Father . . . draw him." The very faith we exercise is graciously granted to us by God. Our conscious experience of committing our lives to Jesus Christ—believing in His death and resurrection and opening our hearts to receive Him—is a consequence of God's sovereign will.

2. To God's gracious love

    a) 1 John 4:19—When you stop to think that you're saved because He predetermined to bring you into an intimate love relationship with Himself, you ought to rejoice. John put it this way: "We love him, because he first loved us." A child gives love to his parents as a response to the love and care that they initially provide. James is making the point that because God has willed to save us and give us new life and a holy nature, it is absolutely incongruous that He would ever lead us into sin.

    b) 1 John 3:1—God predestinated us in love, giving us new life that we might have eternal fellowship with Him. He longs for us to be in His presence where He will further transform us into the image of His Son and pour out eternal blessing on us. It is no wonder John says, "Behold, what manner of love the Father hath bestowed upon us, that we should be called the children of God." No adjective could express that indescribable privilege.

The phrase "of His own will" is a translation of the aorist participle *boulētheis,* implying that regeneration is not just a wish on God's part but an active expression of His will. It is totally unlike our concept of wishing for something that may or may not happen. God's desires are always fulfilled in accordance with His will because He has the power to bring them to pass.

III. THE MEANS OF REGENERATION

A. Stated

James 1:18 tells us that God begot us "with the word of truth." That refers to the Word of God, or Scripture. God regenerates us, cleansing us and giving us a new inner person, through the power of His Word. If people don't hear the message of salvation, then they can't be saved.

B. Supported

1. 1 Thessalonians 2:13—Paul commended the Thessalonians for how they responded to the preaching of God's Word: "For this cause also thank we God without ceasing because, when ye received the word of God which ye heard of us, ye received it, not as the word of men but as it is in truth, the word of God, which effectually worketh also in you that believe." The Word works in conjunction with a believing heart. Salvation takes place when God sovereignly moves to redeem a person who responds to His Word with faith.

2. Titus 3:5—"Not by works of righteousness which we have done, but according to his mercy he saved us, by the washing of regeneration, and renewing of the Holy Spirit." The Spirit works together with the Word in bringing a person to the point of salvation.

C. Specified

Salvation isn't the result of performing religious duties or trying to obey God in the flesh; it's the result of receiving the Word of truth. That particular phrase is used several times in the New Testament.

1. 2 Corinthians 6:7—"*The word of truth,* by the power of God" (emphasis added).

2. Colossians 1:5—"Of which ye heard before in *the word of the truth* of the gospel" (emphasis added).

3. 2 Timothy 2:15—Those who teach the Bible need to be "rightly dividing *the word of truth*" (emphasis added).

The word of truth is not only a general revelation of God's Word that reveals His Person and His will to us but also the more specific revelation of the gospel—the good news that Jesus came, died, and rose again to forgive sin and reconcile us to God.

People are saved when God sovereignly gives them new natures, washing away their sin and planting His Spirit in them when they are prompted to respond in faith to the gospel.

IV. THE PURPOSE OF REGENERATION

A. Identified

You may have wondered why God bothered to save people. Verse 18 tells us it was so "we should be a kind of first fruits of his creatures." That phrase using the Greek particle *eis* with the verb "to be" is a purpose clause, indicating that God saved us for the purpose of producing a new kind of creation.

B. Illustrated

To understand the term *first fruits* we need to study Old Testament passages such as Exodus 23:19, Leviticus 23:9-14, and Deuteronomy 18:4; 26:1-19. When an Israelite planted a crop, God expected the firstfruits of the harvest, meaning two things: the first crops to be harvested and the best fruits available. That demonstrated that an Israelite was to live by faith, for when the farmer took the first portion of his harvest and willingly gave it to the Lord, he would be trusting the Lord to provide more. The natural tendency might be to hoard it in case nothing else came through.

The world will not continue the way it is right now. It is headed for a total transformation. The Bible tells us that the Lord will recreate this earth to His own liking, making a new heaven and a new earth (2 Pet. 3:10-13). A whole new creation is coming, and believers in this age are just the first evidence of it.

In Romans 8 Paul says that the world doesn't even know what we're going to be yet because we're still veiled in our flesh and waiting for the manifestation of the sons of God, when it will become clear what we really are (vv. 19-23). It is exciting to know that as a Christian I am a prototype of what's coming—the first sample of God's new creation. As the firstfruits, we're the promise of the full crop. We are the promise of God's re-creation yet in the future. Paul says that "the whole creation groaneth and travaileth in pain. . . . And not only they, but ourselves also, who have the first fruits of the Spirit, even we ourselves groan within ourselves, waiting for the adoption, that is, the redemption of our body" (vv. 22-23). We're not groaning for the recreation of our souls—that's been done already—but for that of our bodies, which is where our fleshly nature resides. This new life we have in Christ is a taste of future glory when the whole universe will be recreated. What a marvelous privilege!

Regeneration is a sovereign act of God. He mixes our faith in His Word with His sovereign power to transform us. We are living examples of where this world is headed when He re-creates it. James is reaffirming that God does not tempt us to sin. He is never pleased with our sin. Rather He created us to be a model of a sinless society. So when we sin, we must never blame Him. We should put the blame where it belongs: on our flesh. We should also be longing for the day when our bodies will be redeemed along with our souls.

Focusing on the Facts

1. What is necessary for man to have a relationship with God? Support your answer with Scripture (see p. 86).
2. What fact are most people oblivious to? What do the few who aren't oblivious do (see p. 87)?
3. What happens when men divert themselves from the path that God ordained for righteousness (see p. 87)?
4. What does Romans 3:9-18 reveal mankind's standing before God to be? Rather than justifying man, what does God's law do (Rom. 3:19-20; see pp. 87-88)?
5. Why does James introduce the subject of regeneration in 1:18 (see p. 88)?

6. Can man resolve to work his way out of his spiritual deadness? Explain the kind of change man needs in order to enter into a right relationship with God (see p. 89).
7. Why doesn't an unbeliever understand or accept "the things of the Spirit of God" (1 Cor. 2:14; see p. 89)?
8. When we were "dead in sins," what did God do for us (Eph. 2:5-6; see p. 90)?
9. Although he was one of the prominent religious teachers in Israel, what did Nicodemus recognize about Jesus (John 3:1-2; see p. 91)?
10. According to Jesus, what is the only way that a person can enter the kingdom of God (John 3:3; see p. 91)?
11. Explain what Jesus meant by being born of water and the Spirit (see pp. 91-92).
12. Why did Jesus compare the Spirit's saving work to the wind (see p. 92)?
13. From God's standpoint, what is salvation (see pp. 92-93)?
14. What does the phrase "of his own will begot he us" tell us that man needs (v. 18; see p. 93)?
15. Although the actual act of salvation is imperceptible to others, how is it manifested (see p. 94)?
16. Regeneration results from the _____ of the Giver, not the _____ of the receiver (see p. 94).
17. Why should God get all the credit when people are saved (see p. 94)?
18. Although we exercise our wills in receiving Christ, whose will ultimately brings about our spiritual rebirth (John 1:12-13; see pp. 94-95)?
19. What should be our response to God's gracious love? Support your answer with Scripture (see p. 95).
20. Identify the means God uses in regeneration and cite a Bible reference (see p. 96).
21. Identify and explain the purpose of regeneration according to James 1:18 (see p. 97).
22. How does God's purpose make it inconceivable that He would lead us into sin (see p. 98)?

Pondering the Principles

1. Although it may seem like salvation is all God's work, God has in His wisdom included us in the process. Romans 10:13-15

says, " 'Whoever will call upon the name of the Lord will be saved.' How then shall they call upon Him in whom they have not believed? And how shall they believe in Him whom they have not heard? And how shall they hear without a preacher? And how shall they preach unless they are sent?" (NASB). Our responsibility is not to save others; it is to proclaim the gospel and let the Spirit of God do His saving work as He sovereignly chooses. Ask God daily for opportunities to share the Word of truth with relatives, friends, neighbors, or coworkers. Meditate on 1 Corinthians 9:19-23, and follow Paul's example by doing all you can to lead others to Christ.

2. Consider the privilege we have as Christians in being the first-fruits of God's new creation, and thank God for it. Pray that you might shine in the world as a light of truth and hope. Make sure that others see your attitude of gratefulness to God so that they might desire to have the new life and joy that you have been given. If you have blamed God for your sin, confess that to Him, seeking to live a life of holiness in the power of His Spirit. Meditate on Paul's words: "Prove yourselves to be blameless and innocent, children of God above reproach in the midst of a crooked and perverse generation, among whom you appear as lights in the world, holding fast the word of life" (Phil. 2:15-16, NASB).

Scripture Index

Topical Index